The Skeptic's Apprentice

The Skeptic's Apprentice

ASTONISHMENT AT THE CRUMBLING EDGE OF REALITY

James Vincent Plath

ISBN: 0692696776
ISBN 13: 9780692696774
Library of Congress Control Number: 2016912119
Dharma Lion Press, New York, NY

Table of Contents

Read this book
and then burn yourself up
in the fires of contemplation.

Dream Dialogue One

⚜

Randi and I are sitting in a restaurant in Hawaii. (But it isn't a restaurant. And we aren't in Hawaii.)

Randi: (smiling) Jimmy, I can't believe that we're in Hawaii!

Me: But we're not, Randi. We're in New York. In my apartment.

Randi: We *are* in Hawaii, Jimmy. Certainly we're in Hawaii!

Me: We are not.

Randi: Though I must say, these are just about the weirdest seat cushions I've ever sat on. Very thin!

Me: Well, that's because they aren't seat cushions. They're maps, Randi. *You are actually sitting on a map of Hawaii!*

Randi: Hmm. This is a very strange restaurant, indeed.

Me: How do you like the food? Delicious?

Randi: No, no, it's terrible. It tastes like cardboard!

Me: Well, maybe it tastes that way because you're eating the menu, my friend.

Randi: (spits out chewed pieces of the menu onto the table)

Me: (wiping the corner of my mouth with a napkin, smiling) You should try the meal sometime, Randi.

Check!

CHAPTER 1
Meeting the Master

❧

THE BEGINNING

MY STORY BEGINS IN THE great state of New York. I was born in Brooklyn to the most loving woman in the world, Carmela and to the toughest man I've ever met, Frank Plath. Carmela was going to be, of all things, a nun. Frank was a numbers runner, a street hustler, a real knock around guy. She was the incarnation of pure selfless love. He was a lot like Tony Soprano. Just rougher.

But the tough guy had a colossal heart and they fell in love and out I came: tossed mercilessly onto this great strange stage of confusion.

I was raised as a Catholic, but was quickly kicked out of religion class for asking one too many skeptical questions. The one that got me booted was a good one: Who made God? My religion teacher couldn't answer that one and so she sent me packing. It was probably for the best.

My parents raised me to have a deep reverence for nature and science and a tremendous love of reading. Every Saturday, without fail, my mother and brother and I would take the bus to the Patchogue-Medford Public Library and I would return home with a stack of treasures. For free! Besides the great books, the other treat was that on those library days we were allowed to get a slice (or two!) of pizza and an ice cold Pepsi a few doors down from the library. Trust me when I tell you that if you've never had New York pizza, you're missing out.

In the end, though, it was always all about the books. How I loved and still love books. I love the feel of them, the smell of them, everything

3

about them. I bet you feel the same, dear reader, as you are right now reading this. I think you will really love it, this ride we're about to embark on together, just you wait and see.

My mother's stack of books always had some real heavy hitters included in it. She would take home passionate, heavyweight minds like Soren Kierkegaard, Friedrich Nietzsche, Martin Buber and Thomas Merton, just to name a few. My mom would keep her books on our kitchen corner table and I would gaze at the titles she had chosen with such longing, wishing I only had the understanding to read them, but knowing that I was far too young at the time. I remember skimming through her books and seeing so many sagely and enigmatic words. What in the world were they saying?

I knew that there was profound stuff stacked up high there in our kitchen. Would there be an answer to the question as to where both of my grandmothers went when they died? Or both of my grandfathers, who I had never even met, because both had died before I was born? Even at that very young age, I craved for immortality. I knew that the world might be a frightening place, but I also knew that I didn't want to leave it.

I knew right then and there standing in that kitchen that I didn't want to lose my mother and father and my brothers and sister and all of those that I loved. Most of all I knew that I didn't want to lose my *own* self. I didn't want my own consciousness to cease forever. That thought haunted me many a night. Yes, I would gaze at my mother's philosophical books and quietly sit there in the kitchen with the tombstone blues.

PHILOSOPHY BEGINS IN DISAPPOINTMENT

Around this time I discovered philosophy, magic and the art of sleight of hand. From a very young age I wanted to do *real magic*. I tried and failed over and over again. It just didn't work! I quickly learned that there wasn't such a thing as breaking the laws of physics, so I settled for sleight of hand and the art of conjuring tricks.

One of my all-time favorite philosophers, Simon Critchley, once wrote that philosophy begins in disappointment. So it goes. I went out and bought a top hat and cape and a deck of cards and declared to my family and friends that I was an existential magician. I was twelve years old.

One day I asked my parents if they would please take me to a magic shop. They just looked at each other and smiled and then my dad said let's take a ride to Port Jefferson. The magic shop was big and mysterious and had all sorts of strange masks and novelty items and best of all it was teeming with magic tricks. The owner, Ronjo, was very nice and he gave me personal attention and was just so wonderful to both me and my parents.

I will never forget the moment when he made a small red ball vanish into thin air, only to have it reappear seconds later, stuck to the ceiling high above my head. That was it. I was hooked. I bought my very first trick (a set of four of those magical red sponge balls) and began a life of magic and wonder that continues to this day.

SUPER MAGIC

By the age of fifteen I had found the two people, both world famous and extraordinary magicians, who would become lifelong heroes of mine. One was the brilliant magician Paul Harris, who many consider to be the greatest card magician of all time and a true innovative genius. I devoured book after book by Paul Harris, every one of them jam-packed with magical ingenuity. The ideas that he had created were beyond anything my young and voracious mind had ever witnessed.

To this day I have never seen anyone handle a deck of cards like Paul Harris. On guitar, Eddie Van Halen is the joyous wizard of the fret board and Paul Harris is the Eddie Van Halen of card magic. One of his books in particular, *Super Magic*, changed my life. This was a work of pure genius filled to the brim with far out, mind twisting ideas and beautiful, entertaining routines. There still isn't any magic book like it. Paul Harris made me want to quit high school and be a true magical artist.

THE AMAZING ONE

The other guy was James "The Amazing" Randi, the world's greatest escape artist since Houdini, who is an incredible magician and a heroic combatant of fraudulent psychics and other bizarre claims. The Amazing Randi was billed as *The Man No Jail Could Hold* and he was able to somehow escape from handcuffs, chains, ropes, jails-- just about anything. He even escaped from a straightjacket while hanging upside down high over Niagara Falls! A very mysterious fellow indeed.

James Randi also seemed to know everything. Smart? He had a 168 IQ (off the charts!) and was very well read in many subjects, such as physics and astronomy, just to name a few. Randi's good friends were many of the geniuses of the twentieth century, including the Nobel Prize winning physicist Richard Feynman, the prolific author and scientist Isaac Asimov, the famous astronomer and creator of the Cosmos series, Carl Sagan, and the great writer Martin Gardner.

It also helped add to his mystique that Randi looked like a true wizard with his long white beard and equally bushy and skeptical eyebrows. This is the man who famously busted the psychic Uri Geller and hundreds and hundreds of other con artists who preyed on a gullible public. Randi is also the guy who single handedly took down the fraudulent faith healers and was granted the MacArthur Genius Award for his great work.

During one of my weekly library visits with my mother and brother I checked out a paperback book called *The Magic of Uri Geller* by James Randi. This book had such an effect on me that I really did consider quitting school. I didn't like how the teachers were teaching at all. There was no soul to their teachings, no instilment of wonder, no fire in their eyes. *The Magic of Uri Geller* also included, on the very last page, a challenge

Randi had issued to all psychics. Randi offered to pay ten thousand dollars to anyone who could demonstrate the existence of paranormal powers under proper observing conditions. At the bottom of the challenge was Randi's full home address, in Rumson, New Jersey. Hmm...

SCATTERING JOY

At school, I was on fire with my reading and magic and was also a big hit in the school cafeteria. I was a little shy, so my classmate Nicky Garone, who wasn't shy at all and loved my magic, would bang his hand loudly on the table and shout out that it was magic time! My fellow students and friends would come running over and Nicky would just smile excitedly and say to me, Go get them, buddy! Knock 'em dead!

That was my cue to whip out my trusty pack of playing cards and those red sponge balls and some coins and go to work, razzling and dazzling my classmates with magic, much of it inspired by Paul Harris and his amazing books. It was a joy for me to make those kids happy and believe me, this was no easy crowd to please. The angles in that cafeteria were atrocious. I had students in front, in back, next to, and practically in my pockets. I was totally surrounded and the only crowd control I had was good old Nicky, beaming. This was where I learned to hone my craft, where I learned to deal with any angle and any situation and be able to pull off some amazing feats. It also taught me to be the best in the world, no matter what the circumstances were. To deliver the goods.

Best of all, to scatter joy!

Eventually, I decided that high school just wasn't for me. The teachers weren't teaching curiosity of knowledge, they were just ploughing ahead through the readings, many of them teaching the same thing year after year. I needed some time to get away and to create something new. I felt suffocated and I knew I had to get out and be free. I even started to cut classes, cleverly sneaking past the guards like Houdini and walking up to the main road to take the bus to the magic shop.

There, or at the library, I felt completely at home. There in the magic shop or the library I was surrounded by mystery and I felt a strong pull towards wonder.

Little did I know what really was behind that pull.

I talked my parents into allowing me to leave school with the promise that I would return shortly. I just needed to be alone and to create at my own pace and do my own thing. I met with my guidance counselor, Mr. Baglio, who in a last ditch effort, tried to talk me out of leaving school. He was a real nice guy, but he just didn't get it. He thought I was throwing my life away. He said, You want to be a what? A magician?

Mr. Baglio smiled and reached into his pocket and came out with a shiny quarter and flipped it to me across his big desk. He told me to go and buy a newspaper and then come back and show him all the jobs listed in the classified section for magicians. He laughed. I held the quarter in the palm of my hand for him to see, then slowly closed my fingers around it. I told him to watch as I gently blew on my hand. Again, slowly, I opened my hand, finger by finger.

It was totally empty! His quarter had vanished into thin air. Gone! I smiled and looked him directly in the eyes. His eyes and mouth were wide open, in complete amazement. There would be no more words from him. I told him I'd be back in the winter and threw him a wink and was out the door in a flash. Gone!

So that September, as eleventh grade was just heating up and just shy of my sixteenth birthday, I asked my loving mother to put pen to paper and to sign me out of school. I needed the freedom to read what I wanted, at my own faster pace, plus the freedom to create on my own, and to just burn, burn, burn. School was completely stifling that. Believe it or not, I did have a plan. I'd leave in September and come back in January after the holiday break. Then I would double up and take twelfth grade during the summer and graduate early. My parents reluctantly agreed. They trusted that I knew what I was doing.

At home, I slept upstairs in our half-finished attic and so as to not have any bad influence on my younger brother, Rob, I would stay quiet on school mornings, not moving or making a sound until he left for middle school. This ensured that he would think that I had already left for school every day before him and arrived home before him, too. I did this for four months. Rob never said a word about it, so the plan worked!

As soon as my brother had left for school and I heard the front door shut, I bolted downstairs and gobbled up some breakfast and read something amazing while I ate. Then, it was on! It was Michael Jordan time for me. It was Eddie Van Halen time. This meant it was time to put in the 10,000-20,000 hours and become a true master. As Salvador Dali wrote, to become a genius, one must play at being a genius. I played hard. It was time to learn as much as humanly possible and also to work as hard as I could on my magic skills and read everything I could get my hands on concerning philosophy, psychology, anthropology, cosmology, the neurosciences, art, literature, world masterpieces, poetry, and plays. The works!

Those few months off were such a creative time for me. During my self-imposed exile, I even dared to pen a letter to The Amazing Randi himself, telling him how much I admired him and asking for magic lessons at our house. In return, because I was just sixteen and penniless, I vowed to him that as payment my parents would cook him marvelous meals of delicious Italian and German food.

Hey, it was worth a shot, right?

SHIELDS AND SCHULZ

This wasn't my first foray into reaching out to my heroes by mail. I had already written to the pretty model and actress Brooke Shields and also to Charles Schulz, the creator of *The Peanuts* cartoons. Now Brooke Shields was no hero of mine. She was more like a muse. I wrote her a really nice letter after seeing her on television and told her how beautiful she was and that I had this crush on her. She was kind enough to send me a colorful postcard thanking me for my interest. It didn't take a rocket scientist to realize that it was only a form letter reply that she probably sent out to everyone who had bothered to write her, but that was okay with me. I really enjoyed the picture of her on the front of the postcard, featuring Brooke lying on the floor looking up at me in her skin tight Calvin Klein jeans. So what if it was a form letter? The only form I cared about back then was her's in those form fitting jeans. Hey, I was a healthy, growing boy. I tucked Brooke under my pillow and slept well.

Charles Schulz was a different story. He really did write me back. Shortly after writing him, I received a note written directly to me, even quoting details of my letter. I knew this to be the case, because I had sent him a drawing of Snoopy that I had done by hand and asked him for a job! Charles Schulz wrote me back saying that he pretty much had Snoopy and the Peanuts gang covered, although he did like my picture and that I did draw a really good Snoopy. His advice to me was that I should create something new, something of my own.

POSTCARD FROM THE EDGE

A few weeks after I had written that letter to Randi, a postcard arrived in the mail. Like the Brooke Shields postcard, this postcard also had a picture on the front. Thankfully, unlike Brooke's postcard, The Amazing Randi wasn't pictured lying on the floor in a pair of skin tight Calvin Klein jeans! This postcard featured a huge black and white photo of The Amazing Randi's face, with his famous long white beard and raised eyebrow. I slowly flipped over the card and read it.

> *Hi Jimmy. While I can't visit you out on Long Island, you are welcome to come here and visit me in New Jersey.*

Wait. What!

I quickly flipped back to The Amazing Randi's face. That beard! That eyebrow! His intense and penetrating skeptical stare. Both of my eyebrows raised in amazement. I read on. It said that he was going to be away for most of November and December, but that he would return home for the holidays in late December and he asked for me to pick a day and to please give him a call to confirm.

What a way to cap off my self-imposed high school sabbatical! There, at the bottom of the postcard, he had written his home phone number. This was no form letter, ladies and gentlemen. This was the real deal. My heart was pounding as I read it over and over again, all alone in the house. In true Zen fashion, I didn't waste any time. I called and got Randi's machine and left a message, choosing December 26th, the very next day after Christmas.

When that day finally arrived, was I ready. I had practiced and read for ten hours a day, every day, leading up to the holidays. Just to be on the safe side, my parents sent me off to New Jersey with my older brother, Frankie. Frankie was a bricklayer and tall and tough like my father. My parents knew that no one was going to mess with me or hurt me with Frankie around. Frankie and I had a fun talk on the train ride to Jersey and I could tell even Frankie was excited to meet The Amazing One!

HOPE IS THE THING WITH FEATHERS

As our train slowly pulled into the Red Bank, New Jersey train station on that blistery winter day, all we could see was a sea of people, all trying to get somewhere for the holidays. I nervously asked Frankie how were we ever going to find Randi in the enormous crowd. After all, Randi had no idea what I looked like. But then, I spotted it! *It* was a huge colorful feather, at least two or three feet in length, moving through the ocean of people. What was the meaning of this? It was very strange indeed. Could it be? Nah, it just couldn't be.

Or could it?

I nudged my brother to look in the direction of this mysterious feather and together Frankie and I watched the vibrant feather make its way through the bustling crowd. And then, just like that, we saw it.

The feather was attached to a big black felt hat and the big black hat was perched atop of the head of a very short, white-bearded man with glasses. The Amazing Randi! It was him! In the flesh!

Riding Shotgun with James Randi

We jumped off the train and I grabbed a hold of Frankie's hand and we made a beeline for that feather. After some creative maneuvering through the crowd, suddenly there he was, standing right in front of us, those bright blue eyes of his twinkling, just like Kris Kringle on the day after Christmas.

Introductions were made and then Randi whisked us away in his Volvo. What he kept forgetting was that this Volvo actually wasn't *his* Volvo, but rather his son's Volvo (they owned matching ones). He informed us that this one, his son's, was souped up. It was extra fast, as we would soon find out!

So there we were, flying through the streets of Rumson, New Jersey with Randi telling us all sorts of stories and every now and then forgetting it wasn't his car and so tapping that gas pedal a little extra, sending us soaring and sometimes leaving the ground for a second or two and coming down hard with a thud to his dismay, as our car roared towards The Amazing Randi residence.

What a ride and a fun time we had on that drive with Randi. During the ride, Randi told us that his house was actually purchased from a Sears catalog. What! I couldn't help but imagine what this mysterious house might look like. Would it have secret passageways and bookcases that opened into hidden rooms with a wave of his hand? We were flying through the back roads, my brother in the backseat, me riding shotgun and The Amazing Randi at the wheel. *Don't* be careful for what you wish for, you may get it! It has been some journey and we are still only at the very beginning. Don't worry, we're just laying the groundwork. Be patient, enjoy the ride, for soon we will arrive at true astonishment beyond words.

Back in Jersey, we pulled up to the house and I noticed on the lawn near the front of the porch a big sign that read *Professional Charlatan*. Randi introduced us to his cat Charles and to his talking parrot, Fred. What a day we all had together. We spent hours and hours discussing magic and philosophy and watching magicians on video and Randi showed me his library and his magic collection.

At one point Randi waved his hands at a bookcase and it mysteriously opened into a secret room. There, in the room, standing right before me, was Houdini's original Milk Can Illusion. I was blown away. I ran my fingers over the can, inspected the locks, and knocked on its side. Amazing. Houdini's actual handmade illusion! Randi sat with me and we had hot chocolates and discussed the meaning of life. I told him I was an atheist. I told him that the evidence for science was far greater than the minuscule evidence for the existence of a god. He smiled and said I was right and that he felt the same way. We both agreed that we humans were responsible for bringing meaning into our lives and that consciousness ceased at death.

Frankie joined us now and then or he read on the couch and smoked cigarettes outside on the porch. I'm so glad Frankie went with me. I felt safe and it was nice of him to give me all of his time that day, allowing me to spend hours with my hero. He was selfless, like my mother and my sister Barbara, all gentle people with big hearts.

BACK TO SCHOOL

As the day came to a close, after many amazing hours with The Amazing Randi, we said our goodbyes. Randi gave me a gift, a poster he had personally signed to me, one with a picture of him performing the milk can escape on it, entitled *The Amazing Randi: The Man No Jail Could Hold*.

I couldn't wait to hang it up in my attic room for inspiration. On the train ride back I mostly dreamt of a life in magic, a life spent entertaining people, performing amazing feats of wonder, and most importantly, bringing joy to others. Soon my self-imposed sabbatical was over and I found myself back in high school with my mind on fire with creativity and excitement. I was unsure just how I would be accepted when I came back, but my classmates were very cool to me, welcoming me with open arms and begging for "Magic time" again and again in the cafeteria.

LESSON ONE

Randi and I stayed in close touch and we would talk on the phone and we would always write great letters to each other. In one of those very first letters, Randi asked me why I liked magic in the first place. I replied that I wanted to do magic because I wanted to make others happy and that I wanted to use magic as a tool to make people feel good and to make them smile. In other words, to scatter joy. Randi's next letter arrived in the mail and this was his response:

You say that you want to do magic to truly make others happy.

Scratch lesson #1 kiddo. You already know it.

It's all about love.

Those words above were very powerful to me and I have kept them with me my entire life. Not only do I reprint them here, but they are now written on my heart.

It's all about love.

Those words also play a huge role in this book, as the reader will soon see after chapter three!

Interesting little fact: Both Paul Harris and James Randi, although born many years apart, share the very same birthday. Both of these amazing men were born on August 7th!

Florida Bound

One day I wrote Randi and told him I just couldn't work a regular job anymore, as my parents wanted. I told him that I didn't want to conform and be a robot like everyone else. I couldn't do it. I just wanted to learn about the world and share my magic and make others happy. Two letters arrived just a few days later. Both from Randi. Two!

I opened one and read it slowly. Tears ran down my face. Randi told me that my parents wanted these things because they loved me. They wanted me to be happy and to be secure with a good job and a future. He said that there is comfort to be found in being in the herd. That was why they wanted me to be like others, it was safer to be a part of the herd. But, I should also be given the chance to follow my own star. He then said that he wanted to make me the following offer:

> *Jimmy, I'm preparing to move to Florida and you're welcome to come and stay there with me as my apprentice.*
>
> *You'll have your very own room, no rent to pay, and you will be free to pursue your dream and to follow that star...*

The Skeptic's Apprentice

I was floored. My heart was pounding. But wait, there was still that other letter to open! Now I was worried that the second letter would say forget the previous offer, that he's reconsidered. He had to have made a mistake. It was too good to be true. I opened letter number two and once again read it slowly.

In this letter, Randi detailed what an enormous undertaking this would be for him. He explained that this was no easy thing to do, opening his home to an apprentice, that he had tried this before and he had been burned. One guy had robbed him and cleaned out his bank account. Another had brought drugs into his home. Randi said that he wanted to help me out and that he saw a lot of promise in me. He said he didn't think I would do anything bad and that he trusted me, but he wanted to let me know that this was a big deal for him.

> *But that said, we should give it a try. Buy a plane ticket and come on down to Florida in a few months!*

> *-Randi*

And so began the adventure of a lifetime.

STUDYING WITH THE WORLD'S GREATEST SKEPTIC

I studied closely with Randi, learning all about the physical universe, about the building blocks of matter, the atoms, and about protons and electrons and quarks and the big stuff like the stars and the quasars and black holes and galaxies. It was all so mind blowing. His close friends were the giants in the fields of physics and chemistry and biology, from Isaac Asimov to Richard Feynman to Carl Sagan to Richard Dawkins. Randi knew them all very well and I was soon learning from them and their books and coming to understand how the universe operated from the very small scale all the way up to the billions of galaxies swirling out there in the deep space of the cosmos. I was what you would call a strict reductionist materialist and very proud of it. I thought I had a firm handle on the truth. All of us skeptics did.

I had my own room in Randi's amazing new house in Sunrise, Florida. He set me up with a beautiful chess set and plenty of books and some nice plants. Every day I would go down and feed Fred, Randi's talking bird, and I'd pet Charles the cat, and then dive deeply into his immense library. One day while perusing Randi's library I found a book that rocked my world. It was Martin Gardner's classic book *The Annotated Alice in Wonderland*. I felt like I had just struck gold. There was so much wordplay and creativity and riddles to be discovered between those pages. I remember browsing through it and Randi poking his head in and asking what I was reading.

I told him and he said, Ah Martin Gardner, everything that man touches turns to gold, Jimmy.

That stuck with me.

All sorts of interesting people would drop by Randi's house, from world famous scientists to wild looking entertainers, many of them magicians. It was thrilling to be a part of those conversations on life and meaning. I would sit and listen to those amazing minds as they would discuss the latest findings in chaos theory or philosophy of mind or go into great detail about a work of art they had seen or a powerful book they had just read.

I never wanted to leave.

The problem was that I had a girlfriend waiting for me back in New York. Cindy was my first serious girlfriend and we were in love and I missed her terribly. We wrote many letters back and forth and would have long talks on the phone late at night. As much as I loved being at Randi's, I really missed Cindy and my family and friends back in New York. I knew at some point I would have to go back home and informed Randi of this and he said that no matter what my decision was, that we would always stay in close touch and that he felt like a spiritual father to me.

Before I left for New York, we had one last big adventure in Florida together. The phony faith healer Peter Popoff was in town and was appearing at a local auditorium where he promised to heal people of their diseases and ailments by laying his hands on them.

Randi knew that Popoff was a liar and a fraud. Popoff would go into the crowd and somehow know people's names and addresses. He would call these folks out by name and tell them their home addresses and look up to the heavens and would know if they had cancer or cataracts or whatever it was that they were suffering from. He said the knowledge came from God. Randi knew better.

One day at breakfast Randi asked me point blank how Popoff could have known the names, addresses and sicknesses of all of those people. I thought for minute, took a bite of my omelet, and then said confidently that I bet Popoff had some electronic device hidden on him and he was getting the information from a confidant hidden somewhere in the building. Randi smiled, his eyes twinkling more than ever. He said I was right and that he had already put a friend of his, a guy who was a master of electronics, to work on making a scanner that would catch any radio transmissions to Popoff.

Then he said that early the next morning we would go and snatch Peter Popoff's garbage right out of the trash bins and bring it back to our patio and go through it. We'd gather evidence. James Randi did not screw around. He was and still is deadly serious about his work. Being his apprentice, this fierce as fuck attitude rubbed off on me and I learned to be a fearless skeptic, like my mentor.

We arose before dawn and headed out to the facility and surreptitiously grabbed bags and bags of trash and threw them all in the truck and brought them back to Randi's patio and then we meticulously went through it all, with gloves on. Popoff claimed that the letters sent to him, which were always accompanied by checks or cash, were prayed upon backstage and anointed with holy oil. Yep. More like preyed upon. We quickly noticed that the only oil to be found on those letters was McDonald's french fry oil, from the Popoff staff's lunch. Many letters were shredded and the checks and cash removed and kept by Popoff, who didn't pay taxes on a dime of it. He only paid taxes on his claimed yearly salary, which was low. The rest of the money, millions of dollars, was considered a donation to his church. Tax free.

Before I left for New York, Randi started writing a book on the faith healers, exposing their deceptions. He was also up for the coveted MacArthur Genius Grant, which would mean hundreds of thousands of dollars for Randi, helping him to continue his noble work fighting these horrible people who were continuously robbing a naive and vulnerable public.

But I had to go. I missed Cindy. I missed my friends and family. I missed New York. And I missed pizza. I packed and headed home. Looking back, I had learned an awful lot. I learned that the world was purely physical. I learned that there was no such thing as a god or a soul. I learned that consciousness was based in the brain and that when the brain died, I died with it. Thinking that all of the evidence was on my side, I faced this all with courage.

Little did I know that I was wrong! So was Randi and the entire skeptical community that I was a part of and that I loved so much. But I'm getting ahead of myself. We're just about through setting the stage for the discovery of a tremendous mystery that is beautiful beyond words. We're almost there, my dear friend. One more chapter of my story and then things get real good. Promise!

RETURNING HOME

Initially, I didn't tell most of my friends I was coming back home. I only told Cindy and maybe a very close friend or two. This bought me a little more quiet time to stay in and read, read, read. I made it a time where I threw myself as intensely as possible into all the great pursuits. Psychology, philosophy, anthropology, art, literature, the sciences. I soon learned that many years before me the great writer and Buddhist Jack Kerouac would do exactly this in the Beat poet Allen Ginsberg's room at Columbia University. Jack holed himself up in there and just studied and wrote and called it his period of Self Ultimacy.

I took this to heart. And to the extreme.

Reflecting back to that seminal day in Randi's library, I asked my mom if she would please do me a favor (since I wasn't going out in public just yet) and pick up that book I had liked so much. But I couldn't remember the title! The keywords I gave her to give to the librarian were *Alice in Wonderland, Lewis Carroll,* and *Martin Gardner.* I also told her what Randi had said, that everything Martin Gardner touched was gold.

My mom came back with a book that a reference librarian had found for her based on those clues. It wasn't the right book, but it sure was a big one! It was a seven hundred and seventy seven page tome titled *Gödel, Escher, Bach: An Eternal Golden Braid,* by Douglas Hofstadter. Its subtitle was *A Metaphorical Fugue on Minds and Machines Written in the Spirit of Lewis Carroll.*

On the back of the book was a superb blurb written by, you guessed it, the one and only Martin Gardner, wherein Martin declared that the book was a literary event! Another blurb said that Hofstadter's *GEB* was so good that it was without precedent or peer in modern litera-ture. It had also won the Pulitzer Prize. I looked at this amazing book and flipped through it and fondled it and just knew it was a work of genius.

Its crux was *what is the meaning of the word "I"?* What was a "self"? How does consciousness arise from three pounds of meat? I held on to it for a bit, but ultimately returned it to the library, knowing full well that I wasn't ready for it quite yet. But I vowed to myself that someday I would tackle it.

Boy, did I ever. You wait and see!

Those days were filled with more and more reading and studying, lots of practicing, honing my sleight of hand skills, and inventing things in magic no one has ever dreamt of, still to this day. I was always very proud of that. I was happy. I was excited. Exuberant! But in the back of my mind I was still haunted by the thought *what good was all of this if we just die someday?* Just turn blue and rot in the ground. I could not accept that consciousness, *my precious consciousness*, would suddenly come to a complete stop. That I'd be buried and silenced.

Forever.

What was the point of it all? I was smiling, but always, always haunt-ed by thoughts of mortality. By a tragic sense of life. Was the point of life really that life was truly pointless?

THE DHARMA LION

It was around this time that I would meet another hero of mine, Jack Kerouac's best friend, the wonderful poet, Allen Ginsberg. My brother Rob was a graduate student at Brooklyn College and Allen Ginsberg was one of his teachers. It was wild that I studied with The Amazing Randi and Rob studied with Allen Ginsberg. Two bearded intellectual giants!

As my brother's first semester with Ginsberg came to a close, Allen threw a holiday party for his students and said that they could bring a guest. Rob asked me and our good friend Bill McSherry if we would like to go and we both jumped at the chance. Bill was one of the smartest and most creative guys we knew and we were both ecstatic to meet the wise professor and poet.

The Brothers Plath had great love for the writings of Allen Ginsberg and Jack Kerouac. They had changed our lives. Before going to college was even an idea in our heads, we would spend our summers reading the Beat Generation writers and then diving into Shelley and Byron and Wordsworth and Blake after learning that the Beats were inspired by the Romantics. *Howl*, Ginsberg's powerful poem, had blown me away. Now I would meet the man himself!

Rob and I would spend many days sitting and dreaming and imagining what we would someday contribute to the world. As Walt Whitman wrote, *the powerful play goes on and we can contribute a verse.* I had my magic and writing and Rob was becoming a poet himself. What would our verses be?

Our friend Bill was an amazing guitarist and had a deeply roaming mind. Many a night Bill and I would sit in his room and drink straight vodka with beer chasers and discuss the ideas of Douglas Hofstadter and Salvador Dali and Albert Einstein and the greats, trying to figure out the whole amazing mystery of existence, and later me jamming wild sleight of hand magic ideas along to his incredible guitar work.

The day arrived and we three took the train into New York City and headed over to Ginsberg's apartment in the village. We drank and smoked and talked along the way, excitedly discussing The Beats and Bob Dylan and The Beatles and Timothy Leary and psychedelics and the wild consciousness expanding time of the 1960's, much of it spearheaded by this big-hearted Buddhist poet named Allen Ginsberg.

Malt Liquor

Soon, very soon, we'd be in the presence of one of the greatest poetic minds of the 20th Century. I went into a deli in SoHo and bought the largest beer I could carry (outside of a keg!), sixty four beautiful ounces of ice cold deliciousness. It was malt liquor, but to me, it was heaven.

We found Ginsberg's apartment and rang the bell and soon right there in front of our naked steaming eyes was The Dharma Lion himself, bearded like Randi, bespectacled, and smiling. Allen Ginsberg was standing there in his great doorway. What have you got there in the bag, he asked me. I smiled. Get a load of this Mr. Ginsberg, I said, as I pulled the monster beer out of the big paper bag in a style only a magician can manage.

It was a sixty four ounce rabbit popping out of a paper hat. Voila!

Allen shook a finger at me and said that his party was alcohol free, there was absolutely no drinking. I looked at him, amused.

You *are* Allen Ginsberg, yes? Allen, always getting naked, finger cymbal playing, Ginsberg?

Allen, LSD taking, pot smoking, always naked, Ginsberg, am I correct? *The* Allen Ginsberg? Yes? I asked, grinning.

Always be Drunk!

Allen then smiled his great bearded smile and said it was okay, I may bring it in, and told us that he made a huge pot of soup. Rob knew almost everyone and introduced us and he was very buzzed and very relaxed and chanted aloud about twenty times that night Charles Baudelaire's great poem titled *Always be Drunk*.

> *You have to be always drunk. That's all there is to it—it's the only way. So as not to feel the horrible burden of time that breaks your back and bends you to the earth, you have to be continually drunk.*
>
> *But on what? Wine, poetry or virtue, as you wish. But be drunk.*

And if sometimes, on the steps of a palace or the green grass of a ditch, in the mournful solitude of your room, you wake again, drunkenness already diminishing or gone, ask the wind, the wave, the star, the bird, the clock, everything that is flying, everything that is groaning, everything that is rolling, everything that is singing, everything that is speaking. . .ask what time it is and wind, wave, star, bird, clock will answer you: "It is time to be drunk! So as not to be the martyred slaves of time, be drunk, be continually drunk! On wine, on poetry or on virtue as you wish."

WASHING DISHES WITH ALLEN GINSBERG

Needless to say, that night was one of the greatest nights of my entire life. As luck would have it, after dinner I found myself in the kitchen with Ginsberg, alone. Just the two of us. He was doing the dishes and asked if I wanted to help dry them.

Sure, Allen Ginsberg, I said, and joined him by the sink. Together we talked philosophy and literature and art and he was just so kind, so gentle, and so caring. While we were talking and washing the dishes the Buddhist idea of mindfulness flashed through my mind. One must practice mindfulness when walking, when sitting, when at work, when eating, or after a meal, and while cleaning the dishes.

As the great Thich Nhat Hanh would say, if you're washing dishes then washing dishes should be the most important thing in your entire life. Stay in the moment. Be present. Stay in the now. It's all there is. At one point I asked Allen if he believed in God and he said no, he did not, but that he did believe in karma. I looked at him puzzled and asked him what he meant by karma?

He said wait right here and I watched him sprint into the other room and scale a ladder in seconds and pull a large Buddhist dictionary off of the top shelf and bring it back to the kitchen table.

I'll show you just what I mean, Allen said. Let's see, karma, karma... ah, there it is. And together we read the definition of karma from this great big Buddhist book and we discussed the pursuits of goodness, of compassion, and generosity.

It all made sense to me for the first time.

MEDITATION

Towards the end of the party we all gathered around Allen in the living room and he recited poetry and talked to us. My brother, after yet another joyful recitation of Baudelaire, told him that I was a magician and Allen asked if I would show him a trick. I produced a deck of cards and starting cutting them at lightning speed in both hands and then made a huge beautiful fan and asked Allen to pick any card he wanted and return it to anywhere he wanted in the deck.

He did just that and I shuffled the cards and said "Watch this!" and with a magical flourish one card shot out of the deck, spinning high into the air, making a big rainbow-like arc over Ginsberg's head and headed towards my other free hand, all the while still spinning. I caught the card with that free hand.

Allen squealed. He said that was amazing. I said yes, but look-- and turned it over and it was Allen's chosen card! He was delighted. The students all cheered and howled. Yes, howled.

My brother shouted, Always be drunken, on wine, poetry, or *magic*!

Allen then asked me if I was happy doing magic and I told him yes, that I really enjoyed bringing wonder to others. He then asked me if I had ever meditated. I told him that this was my meditation and launched into a series of very fast one handed cuts, making a circular motion with my hands, hypnotically. I told Allen that I would lose myself in the card cuts and flourishes for hours and that kind of practice was like a meditation. The self vanished or at least felt like it did. When that happened, there was a peaceful feeling. Then Allen Ginsberg said something I'd never forget.

He winked at me and said that someday I would really meditate. Someday, he said again.

I smiled back at him and said yes, someday, not really thinking anything of it. Not realizing that one day that someday would really arrive. And that I would then be in the perfect position to uncover an ancient mystery that would transform this world forever.

Dream Dialogue
Two

❦

Randi: I don't drink, I don't smoke, and I don't do drugs, because I want to be as certain of reality as I possibly can be.

Me: That is very admirable, Randi. But maybe, even after all that, we and our fellow skeptics have missed something. Something big!

Randi: (his world famous eyebrow raised) Oh really? Like what?

Me: Take the matter of matter, for instance. What if we made a bad assumption from day one? A very wrong one?

Randi: I'm listening...

Me: What if we were to take our skepticism to its natural end? What if we're assuming the presence of matter, but, as a matter of fact, there isn't any matter at all?

What if the very idea of a material world is merely a deeply embedded superstition? A superstition to be debunked!

Randi: (reaching for his cane, which is always close by)

Me: Easy now, my man, hear me out. What if, what if we blew it early on?

(knocks on the table)

Look, would you agree that this here table is 99.9% empty space?

Randi: Yep. I'll give you that!

Me: Okay, good. What about that other 0.1%? What *is* that 0.1%?

And *where* did it come from?

How do we get all of this apparent solidity, because that's what it is, *apparently solid, merely an appearance*, from this 0.1%?

What if that final 0.1% is simply a vibration of empty space which sort of looks solid, like a ripple on a pond.

Randi: Well, physics tell us that...

Me: But what if physics, what if YOU have a confirmation bias? You think that matter is prior to consciousness, but what if it's really the other way around? What if prior to the appearance of matter is consciousness?

Randi: No, no, no, Jimmy, consciousness first?

Me: Yes, yes, yes! What if matter is merely provisional, an illusion of consciousness! Physics taken all the way to its end simply reveals what contemplatives, sages, and mystics have known all along!

Randi: (raises his cane, shaking it menacingly)

Suddenly, Randi awakens in his bed. He was merely dreaming! He chuckles and gets dressed.

❦

CHAPTER 2

The Other Side of the Coin

❦

SCHOPENHAUER'S GOLD COIN

LEGEND HAS IT THAT WHEN the virtuoso philosopher Arthur Schopenhauer would visit his much loved restaurant, the *Englischer Hof,* that he would place a gold coin beside him on his table. When he had finished eating his meal and was ready to leave, Schopenhauer would then pocket the coin. He did this every day.

The meaning of this was simple. If the philosopher heard a conversation at another table that he thought had substantial value, one where the men, mostly soldiers, chatted of anything but women, horses or the chances of a promotion, he would give the coin away to charity.

He never parted with the money.

Speaking of food, we're almost there. Here comes the good stuff, the food for thought. But first, you're about to meet a cast of characters that are as intelligent, witty, and as wonderful as anyone on this planet. Just a tiny bit more setting of the table. Then, my friend, you are in for a feast. Are you just about ready?

Don't forget to wash your hands before and when you do make sure you wash them like it is the most important thing in your whole life. Stay present. In the moment. Soon we will unveil the mind blowing reason why the moment matters so much.

COLLEGE BOUND

In college, I majored in Psychology with a double minor in Philosophy and English Literature. I was studying real hard and had drifted away from the magic a little bit, so one day, on a whim, I decided to drop in to my beloved Ronjo's Magic Shop, totally unannounced.

I was excited to see Ronjo and the whole gang at the shop. I walked in and there they all were, smiling at me. It felt like home. Ron was beaming and saying "I told you so" to Pete and the others and then he said to me that he knew I was coming that day!

We were waiting for you, he said.

My eyebrow shot up, Randi-esque. *I* didn't even know that I'd be there. This visit was pure chance. I told him so.

Nope, I knew, he shot back, smiling knowingly. Then my good friend Pete turned over a flyer on the counter and pushed it towards me.

It read: *Paul Harris Lecture. Don't miss it!*

I checked the date. It was the very next day! I couldn't believe what I was seeing. I really had no idea. I paid the money and got my ticket and said goodbye and just left. No looking around, no socializing. I hightailed it right back to the dorms. I needed to think. To wrap my head around this. And to prepare. To practice. Paul Harris? Here? In New York!

If I had popped in the next day, it would have been the day of the lecture. The very day! Imagine? But what if I had dropped in *two days* later and totally missed it. What were the odds? Remember, this was just before the internet and there was no way of knowing that one of my heroes was in town. The mind boggles!

MEETING PAUL HARRIS

In those fun college days I drove an old Volkswagen van I purchased for a few hundred bucks off of my Sociology professor, Jon Fliedner. Big Jon was, I must say, a wild man. Sporting a long flowing white beard, he was tall, would always wear jeans, and wore a bandana around his head. He resembled an intellectual biker Charles Darwin. I approached him on campus one day, not knowing who he was, and exclaimed that I bet he taught Philosophy! Actually, Sociology, he shot back, smiling. I told him that I was definitely taking him my next semester. I just had to. So I did! He was an amazing professor and is a good friend.

The van he sold me was powder blue with a big bright yellow sunset painted on its side with a huge happy face inside the sun and next to the sun in giant letters were the words *BE HAPPY!* People who saw it loved it and would honk and smile at me all the time. The attendant who pumped gas for me at the gas station near the college would always joyously slap the side of the van as loud as he could slap and many a morning before class he would chant "Be happy, be happy, BE HAPPY!" as he happily pumped the gas.

A bodhisattva at the gas pump, indeed!

FUEL

The hippy van also had a refrigerator in it which was always stocked with beer, or as Frank Sinatra called it, fuel. Fuel for what, you may ask? Well, for creating art, of course. Liquid inspiration. A few drinks and a few hours of mindful practice and suddenly wildly creative ideas were flowing like wine. There was also a captain's seat in the back of the van and a couch that pulled out into a bed, with speakers built right into the couch. And curtains, of course, for privacy. It was a party mobile and every cop in town knew it. And so did the college girls. It was a wild time!

I pulled up to Ronjo's shop in the Be Happy Mobile and gunned it into the small lot behind the store. I opened the big side doors, cranked some Van Halen through the stereo speakers, popped open a beer in the captain's chair and started manipulating a deck of cards like it was my last day on this earth. I was flipping packets of cards into the air and catching them in the other hand, like an adventurous bartender would do with bottles, doing wild plasterboard acrobatics and finger flinging and one handed cuts consisting of half the deck in each hand, cutting them at the lightning speed of one hundred and sixty one cuts per minute.

Very, very fast.

Soon the setting sun was upon me and it was time for the lecture. I walked in the front door beaming with excitement and intensity. It was crowded inside, with lots of magicians mulling around, talking to one another, doing tricks with coins, cards and silks.

Showtime!

I walked in and silently mouthed the words "Where is he?" to Brian, who was a fellow magician and good friend who worked for Ronjo.

He's right downstairs, buddy, Brian told me with a smile.

He knew what this day meant to me. I bounded down those stairs two at a time and about halfway down I froze in my shoes.

There he was, in the flesh. Paul Harris!

He was wearing his trademark scarf and there on his face was his great moustache. It was really him. He looked larger than life. I took a seat, front row center, and waited for the lecture to begin. Soon the room filled up and Paul began and was simply amazing, as always. Halfway through we were told there would be an intermission. Bathroom break! I needed one, all that beer! During the break Paul had moved to a table on the side of the room where he had some of his books and effects for sale.

I wanted so badly to go up to him and say hello, but I didn't dare. I took out my cards and showed Brian some of my latest moves and flourishes, all inspired by Paul (and by Eddie Van Halen). Brian was blown away by what he saw and told me Paul must see this and started moving me, physically moving me across the floor, while I was still doing these wild things with the cards, moving me towards Paul Harris.

Paul looked up and Brian said, Mr. Harris, take a look at this.

Now, here I am positioned right in front of one of my idols, a man responsible for inspiring so much of my magic. This was my one shot and

I was determined not to blow it. I was churning the cards at high speed, sailing them from hand to hand in midair, magically. Spectacularly.

I finally said quietly something to the effect of Paul, you inspired all of this.

Paul Harris, smiling, eyes wide, taking it all in, so in the moment, said Hey, who let this guy in here? Then he winked at me. It was the greatest compliment ever.

Paul thanked me for showing him my skills and then I quickly asked him what I'd been waiting to ask him my whole magical life.

Reading your books, and I have read all of them, I get the feeling that you love philosophy. Am I right? I asked him.

Very much so, he replied.

Then again, he repeated it. Very much so.

You couldn't see it at the time, but in my head, I was doing back flips. I told him that I was studying Psychology and Philosophy at Stony Brook University, right down the road. Paul said that was was great and that we should talk more after the lecture. I thanked him and walked back to my seat. It all felt like a dream.

A CARDBOARD CONNECTION

At the end of the lecture, in his very last trick, Paul Harris tore out the centers of two cards and then proceeded to magically link them together. After the trick, he walked over to me in the front row and asked me to hold both of my index fingers up in the air and then he dropped the two cards down onto them like rings and took a bow. I examined them carefully, they were solid, yet they had linked together. We had made a connection.

I still have those two cards.

Afterwards, people hung around a bit, but soon the crowd had thinned and it was getting late so I waited to say goodbye to my hero. In the process of telling him that I was leaving, I showed him a letter from Randi to me and told him that I was Randi's apprentice. Paul was very interested in this and flipped over the envelope and scrawled his address on the opposite side of Randi's. Then he asked me if I'd like to come to dinner with him and Ron and Brian and Ron's sweet wife, Leslie.

I shot a look at Ron as if to ask if this was okay and he said sure.

Alrighty then. *Looks like I'm going to dinner with Paul Harris!*

PORK CHOPS AND APPLESAUCE

Ron closed up shop and we all piled into his car and we headed to a local diner called The Seaport. We started talking and I swear, the whole time, it's just me and Paul Harris discussing philosophy and the meaning of life.

The whole time.

This Paul Harris fellow wasn't kidding around. He was serious.

Do you like philosophy, Paul Harris? Very much so!

At one point I took a shot and asked Paul if he'd ever read Douglas Hofstadter's work. He replied by asking me which book I was referring to and then went on to name all three Hofstadter books that were out at the time: *Gödel, Escher, Bach, The Mind's I,* and *Metamagical Themas.* I was amazed. He smiled. He looked at me as if he was studying me and then asked if he could ask me a question.

Sure, I said. Fire away.

He asked if he could have a bite of my pork chop.

Of course you can, you can have the whole thing, Paul Harris.

He carved off a piece and took a bite and enjoyed it immensely and our conversation continued.

This sentence informs you that I am a vegetarian now.

LESS IS MORE

Paul and I had both read hundreds, maybe thousands of books at that point. I told Paul about my fast growing home library and he smiled and said that he had this fantasy wherein his library bookends would squeeze together and slowly as they squeezed, all of his many books would melt together until there remained only one book left and then with one last squeeze the final book would vanish into nothing.

I admitted that I found this idea strange.

In fact, I hated it. Why in the world would someone want *less* books? Paul said that I reminded him a lot of him when he was younger and that someday, if I was lucky, I would know exactly what he meant by this bookend fantasy. Then he took another bite of my pork chop.

SKEPTICISM

Soon the conversation moved to the nature of skepticism and we discussed Randi and Paul dropped another gem on me that I couldn't understand at the time. He said that he admired Randi a lot and thought he was brilliant, but he felt that Randi wasn't *skeptical enough*.

Huh? Randi was ruthless. Hardcore.

Paul told that me a true skeptic goes all the way with critical thinking and that means questioning the very fabric of space and time. Questioning atoms and solidity and the nature of matter itself. Our conversation was fascinating and challenging and went on and on late into the night. I didn't get home until after 3 a.m., my head spinning with wild ideas and existential reflections. Sadly, after all that, I had zero contact with Paul Harris for many years. Not one word. I wrote to him at his address he left on the envelope, only to learn later that his house had burned down in a California forest fire. His neighbors reportedly said that while they all were in the street looking on sadly, he was serenely smiling while his house was engulfed in flames.

The last I had heard he was living in a park and sleeping on park benches, like a monk.

THE GREATEST MIND SINCE EINSTEIN

In the introduction to his great book *Metamagical Themas: Questing for the Essence of Mind and Pattern*, Douglas Hofstadter wrote about meeting Martin Gardner at Martin's house in New York and what a lovely time he had there discussing ideas with Martin. The philosopher Raymond Smullyan even called Martin while Douglas was sitting there in Martin's study, telling Martin that he was writing a book on Taoism, called *The Tao is Silent*. Douglas recalled how he was astonished that a logician would write a book on such a seeming illogical subject as eastern mysticism.

Martin Gardner was a true skeptic and he was tough on the paranormal, yet he yearned for immortality. Unlike most skeptics I had met through Randi, Martin was not an atheist. He hoped that somehow his consciousness survived death, but he also knew he couldn't prove it. At one point in his introduction, Douglas wrote about all of Martin's friends, great minds from various fields of study. Randi was one of them, of course, with Hofstadter stating that Randi was truly prolific. He then wrote that it seemed like this world of amazing minds all orbited around Martin Gardner.

I was in my teens when I read those words by Douglas in *Metamagical Themas* and I remember telling Randi how much I wished I could be part of such a charmed circle of thoughtful and creative people. I'll never forget Randi's reply. He told me that I already was a part of that very circle because I was his apprentice and very good friend. That hit the teenage me very hard. I was already part of it all, but the others didn't really know it.

Randi said that he knew that someday I would make my presence known.

While I never had the chance to meet Martin Gardner, Randi did show him some of my early writing and then told me that Martin had said it held great promise. Talk about inspiration!

One day I dropped into a bookstore and was browsing the new books and there in front of me was this huge book that caught my eye right away. The font type, the creative cover, the design, it all looked like a Douglas Hofstadter book. I couldn't believe someone had ripped off Hofstadter so blatantly.

The title looked interesting, *Fluid Concepts and Creative Analogies.* Then my eyes dropped down to the author. Douglas R. Hofstadter. Wait. Brand new Hofstadter! I bought it immediately, almost offering cash to a worker who was just stocking the shelves, and for the next few months I savored every word. By the way, that book holds the title of being the very first title ever sold on Amazon.com.

The introduction to this new book wasn't anything like the *Metamagical Themas* introduction. Douglas told the very sad news that his wife Carol had recently passed away due to a brain tumor. This moved me so much that I immediately emailed him and introduced myself and told him just how much he meant to me and how greatly he had shaped my thinking. I told him that I studied with Randi, knowing that he admired Randi a lot and told him that I was thinking of him and that he wasn't alone. I'd always be there for him if he ever wanted a friend. I meant it.

This was the start of an email friendship between us where we shared great ideas and philosophical musings for years. Then one day Doug wrote that he would be speaking at New York's Cooper Union and I got to meet with Doug privately for a few hours and then attend his lecture, front row. It was a dream of a day. Over the years we built a nice friendship, but it was mostly through email. Then one day I sent Doug something that I had read in Carson McCullers' novel, *The Heart is a Lonely Hunter,* that fit his theory of partial survivability between two souls. Heavy stuff. Doug loved it and was very moved. I had sent it to him because not only did it fit his ideas about personal identity and death, but also it reminded me of Doug's tremendous courage to go on writing and living after losing Carol, and to raise his two small children, Danny and Monica, all alone. Many might have thrown in the towel, but I watched my great friend continue writing at such a high level, always creating and passionately pursuing truth and beauty in pure Hofstadterian style.

STRANGE LOOPS

Years later, Doug's secretary Helga Keller, one of the greatest women I've ever met, contacted me and said that Doug would like to use the passage I had sent him a while back for a book that he was writing on consciousness called *I Am a Strange Loop*. Helga asked if I could find it and let her know which novel I had found it in and get its publisher so she could attempt to acquire the rights to use it in Doug's new book.

This meant the world to me because it really drove home how something I had given to Doug, who had given me so much and who had profoundly shaped my mind, had touched him so deeply that he remembered it and wanted to include it in his new book.

I had given something back to my friend.

Well, the new book had me excited, not just because I was *in* it (!), but because it was Doug's return to the subject of philosophy of mind and the ideas he had first shared with the world in *Godel, Escher, Bach*, the book that had started it all for me. Namely, what is this thing called "I"?

Only this time, unlike the books he had written before I knew him, now Doug was writing the book and we were writing each other. I had a behind the scenes look at the creation of *I Am a Strange Loop*. He would tell me about bits and pieces of it and that would inspire me for weeks and months at a time. We even discussed what the cover would look like.

HOFSTADTER: ROUND TWO!

When the book finally came out, Doug came out to New York to speak about it. Actually it was New Jersey, at Rutgers University. Doug told me that he'd love to meet up again and the morning after the lecture would be a great chance for us to catch up and have breakfast. At the time I was dating the girl of my dreams, a beautiful classical pianist named Michele, and we were in love and having the time of our lives together. Michele and I got a hotel right next door to the campus and met Doug after his lecture and I told him how great it was and introduced him to Michele. He was mobbed by people wanting to talk to him so we told him that we'd see him downstairs in the restaurant in the morning.

How's 8:00 a.m.? Doug asked.

Very early, I said. Very, very early.

He laughed. Michele and I smiled.

Well, I do have to leave for a flight back to Indiana. So, early gives us more time, he said.

Ok great. 8:00 a.m. it is, I replied.

Better make it 7:00 am, said Doug, his smile broadening.

What was I going to say? No? Sure, Doug Hofstadter! 7:00 a.m. it is.

So Michele and I enjoyed a fun night in Jersey and somehow, someway, we were up around 6:30 a.m. and we dressed and got ready and headed downstairs to meet Doug Hofstadter for breakfast! Doug came down right on time and we had the nicest breakfast and an enjoyable and fun conversation and then I performed some new magic for Doug. Knocked his socks off. Before we said our goodbyes we gave him a bag of gifts, one being a big Charles Schulz *Peanuts* book and I told Doug about my writing him for a job. Doug got a kick out of that and he said Charles Schulz was one of his favorite people. I also gave Doug a paperback copy of the play *Life Is a Dream*, by Pedro Calderon de la Barca. And a DVD of Stephen Wolinsky, the psychologist who wrote as Doug did about the illusion of a "self" or "I". The title of the DVD was *You Are Not: Beyond the Three Veils of Consciousness.*

I showed Doug the book the DVD was based on, also called *You Are Not*, and Doug asked me to please place that book and his new book next to each other on my bookshelf. This way when looking at them people would see:

I Am a Strange Loop. You Are Not.

Ha!

ON THE ROAD

The following year I decided to take a trip across the country by car, like John Steinbeck. Like Jack Kerouac. I asked Doug if I could stay a few days by him and I'd get a hotel of course. Maybe I could sit in on a few of his classes.

He said yes!

What a time we had together in Indiana. I got to meet his son, Danny and his daughter, Monica. We all hit it off right away. I spent time with Helga and her great husband, Howard. I was treated like royalty, everyone was so nice. Monica took me out to meet Danny for lunch and we all went to dinner every night and had the best talks and of course I performed a lot of my magic. It was a delight! On my very last night there Doug asked me if I'd like to see his study.

Yes, sir!

It was everything I had imagined. So here was where those amazing books were written. This was where many great thoughts were born and then wrestled down onto paper. I snapped a few photos with my phone to remember it. What an ending to my stay. I hugged Monica goodbye and jumped into the car with Doug and Ollie, their loving golden retriever, and we drove back to my hotel. I shook Doug's hand in the car and thanked him for granting me such a dream trip. When I got out and looked back to wave goodbye he was gone.

He'd vanished!

I felt a tap on my shoulder and I spun around and there was Doug in front of me. He had jumped out very quickly and now he stood there smiling, arms wide open and he said come here and gave me a great big hug. What a kind and generous and loving man! I am forever grateful and so honored to be his friend. The next morning I hit the road to California, all the while dreaming of ideas and thoughts about the nature of consciousness and the elusive "I". Much more on this soon!

Over the years our friendship grew closer and closer. Especially when Monica decided to go to school at Parsons College, part of The New School for Social Research here in New York. Perfect choice, Monica! Now I'd get to see Monica and Danny and Charles and their good friends and a lot more of Doug, too. I was even there the day Monica first moved in.

Since then there have been many great dinners and magical late night talks about the meaning of life and art and freewill and consciousness. All of that and just good friendship and lots of puns, jokes and smiles. Speaking of lots of jokes, puns, and smiles, soon I would meet with one of the greatest philosophers alive, a man truly of infinite jest and of most excellent fancy.

⊂⊃

> *Why should I be worried about dying? It's not*
> *going to happen in my lifetime!*
>
> *- RAYMOND SMULLYAN*

TO THE MOUNTAINTOP

One of my all-time heroes is the philosopher Raymond Smullyan. Raymond is an absolute master of logic, so great that Martin Gardner stated that Raymond Smullyan was the best there was at creating and solving fantastic logic puzzles. He is also a Zen master, a dazzling magician, and an incredible classical pianist. Trust me, Dr. Smullyan has one tremendous heavyweight mind.

I read Raymond Smullyan's books during my teens and loved his logic puzzles, but most of all loved his ideas on Taoism, Buddhism, and Zen. Imagine my astonishment when I looked him up one day on Facebook and found him there! Surely a fan page, I thought. He's probably long gone.

I fired off a short message informing the person in charge of his fan page of my love of Raymond's work and how I was a protégé of Randi's, knowing full well that Raymond was a big fan of Randi's work against the fraudulent psychics and faith healers. Not long after I hit send, a message popped up in my inbox from a person claiming to be Raymond Smullyan himself, inviting me up to his house amongst the clouds up high in the Catskill Mountains of Upstate New York.

What? Was this really happening? Oh well, here we go again!

I asked Michele if she would like to take a road trip up to see Raymond Smullyan, the guy we had read together many a night and whose ideas and we had discussed for years. She couldn't believe it! We were both very excited to go see Raymond. Soon we were all packed up and on our way upstate, listening to the beautiful piano music of Douglas Hofstadter the whole ride there. At one point on our journey I called Doug and told him how much we loved him and his music and where we were headed and he was delighted that Michele and I were visiting his longtime friend. Doug said that he knew we would really enjoy Ray and that Ray will just love seeing us.

Lost for a bit, I stopped and asked for directions. We were about five minutes away from the house, according to my calculations, but I couldn't find this one last road to get to Raymond's house. The name of it gave me chills. Plattekill Road. There was *something* about that name that just disagreed with me! This was one of the most dangerous roads in the east, as we would soon find out. I stopped and asked for directions at The Big Belly Deli and a huge guy covered in tattoos and piercings everywhere told me that we were close, just a few turns away. As I

thanked him and turned to leave, he warned me to be careful. He said
Plattekill Road scared the hell out of him.

Uh oh.

HEAVENLY ADVICE

We were almost at Plattekill Road, but I just couldn't seem to find it.
I spotted a church on a corner and saw a priest walking the grounds
outside. I asked Michele to please ask him if we were close to the
road. Michele jumped out and asked and he told her that it was the
next right turn. Excellent! She happily thanked him and just as we
were about to pull away, the priest leaned his entire head into her
open window and looked me in the eye and said, I hope you aren't
scared of heights, son.

I *was* kind of scared of heights. I admit it. I looked at Michele and
nervously smiled as we slowly rolled towards Plattekill Road.

The road was very narrow and we began our climb up the mountain
towards Raymond Smullyan's house. It wasn't just steep, it was *so steep*
that I thought the car was going to flip over like a turtle onto its back.

That steep. I was doing about all of three miles an hour at this
point and we were slowly ascending this insane mountain road, a road
that could barely fit my small Honda Civic, let alone another car coming from the other direction. Then, as if that wasn't enough, the road
became even steeper and incorporated turns in it that were beyond
treacherous. Most of the guard rails were broken and the drop was
unbelievable. Help!

PLATTEKILL ROAD

To be honest, it wasn't all a nightmare. With my heart pounding, I
could see, in quick glances out of the corner of my eye, the most beautiful waterfalls I'd ever witnessed, splashing and hurtling down the
mountain side.

The waterfalls were right next the car, so close that had we chosen to, we could have just reached a hand out of the window and touched the magnificent cascading water. That close! It was beautiful and terrifying. Sublime. Good times! I guess it could have be enjoyable if one wasn't afraid of heights. Or of dying. Or maybe if you weren't afraid of the entire car flipping over and then sailing down off the side of the mountain. Or of the possibility of oncoming traffic that would surely hit you head on and topple you off of the cliff.

I was afraid of all of the above. And then some.

At one point I took a big chance and for a second or two just peeked over out of the corner of my right eye at Michele in the passenger seat and that's when I saw her face, those beautiful eyes wide open, somehow taking in the entirety of the scene, her small talented hands covering her mouth. She was breathless. And breathtaking.

GANDALF ON THE PIANO

Well, we made it through the five minute slow climb up the mountain and the road turned into a normal road and we both let out sighs of relief. My hands were hurting from gripping the wheel so tightly. Soon we arrived at Raymond Smullyan's driveway, which was a few hundred yards long and stretched deep into the surrounding woods.

I rang the bell, but there wasn't an answer. So I rang it again. Again, nothing.

Then we listened quietly and we could hear beautiful piano music coming from inside of the house. It was Bach. I peeked through the curtains on the front door and had Michele take a look, too. There he was, Raymond Smullyan himself, sitting at a gorgeous grand piano and wailing away, his long white hair and his Whitmanesque beard flowing to the music. We just listened for a while and when he came to the end of the piece and stopped I rang the bell for the third time and a few seconds later the door opened wide and I was standing face to face with another of my giants. And he was smiling, happy to see me!

In Sweetness

Raymond invited us inside and then he immediately took hold of Michele's hand and said that he wanted to see if she really was as sweet as I had told him she was. He showed her a quarter and then placed the quarter into his left hand and asked Michele to blow on his hand. She did and presto, he opened his hand and the quarter was gone and had transformed into a packet of sugar! Raymond looked at me and said I was right, she really was sweet!

This was a great start to a wonderful and warm friendship between Raymond and I that continues to this very day. He's still going strong and just published three brand new books a year or so ago at the age of ninety five years old and has published two books already this year at ninety six.

In fact, right now I'm here sitting on Raymond's upstairs outdoor wrap around deck that overlooks the tremendous forest that is his backyard and there are mountains and beautiful deer and I am writing this very sentence that you have just finishing reading!

Ah, is this not happiness?

A Limo?

One day I read that the great philosopher Daniel Dennett would be speaking at my college on Darwin Day. This would be a perfect opportunity to meet him and thank him for all of his brilliant work that I read and enjoyed in the area of philosophy of mind and maybe I could ask him a few things about the meaning of consciousness and the self illusion. I wrote him an email and inquired if this would be at all possible and briefly mentioned that I was Randi's protege.

Well, he replied immediately!

He sent me his itinerary for Darwin Day and asked me to pick a time slot and then to just send it back to him. In good Zen fashion I chose the earliest one, around 9:00 a.m., and thanked him, zapping the itinerary with my choice on it right back to Daniel Dennett.

Here we go again. But wait, it gets even better.

It was a few days before Darwin Day, almost Daniel Dennett time, when an email was sent out to everyone on the Dennett itinerary. Probably just a roll call, I thought. Just a reminder. Wrong!

Apparently Dan Dennett needed a ride from the airport, which was about an hour or more from the campus. I peeked outside and it was stormy as hell and would be for the next few days. I had just purchased my very first brand new car a few months ago and thought, I'm not driving my new car to the airport at night. An airport I'd never been to. Especially in a storm. Definitely not in a storm with the author of the great book *Brainstorms*, Daniel C. Dennett, one of my heroes, riding shotgun.

No way. Too risky.

Yet, I immediately replied to the email, saying sure, if he needs a ride, I can do it. Then I waited! A few hours later, a reply came in. Dr. Dennett's flight and gate information was included. Also included, his cell number and at the bottom a big *"Thank you, James!"*

Looks like I'm picking up Daniel Dennett. I'm now his driver!

Daniel *"Consciousness Explained"* Dennett. Outside of Noam Chomsky, this was arguably the most famous philosopher alive. Yours truly was now responsible for the life of one Daniel C. Dennett. So, what did I do? I called up a limousine company. Could they pick me up and then pick up a new friend at LaGuardia Airport in NY? Their reply: why yes we can.

I booked the limousine and when the day came, I stocked it with a stack of books and three bottles of Smoking Loon wine, which was Eddie Van Halen's favorite libation at the time.

What a ride out to the airport that night, playing Van Halen and Sinatra and drinking Smoking Loon and smoking cigars, the whole while excited to meet another of my lifelong inspirations. Along the way I would tell the driver, Joe, some great stories about Dennett and his wildly philosophical ideas. I showed him a few of his books, too. Even Joe was excited now.

We pulled in and waited in the car by the gate. Not too long after arriving Joe said, I think I see your guy right now.

What's he look like, I asked?

Tall, with a long white beard, glasses. Big guy! In a long overcoat.

That sounds like him, I said, rolling down the window. I spotted Dennett standing there. Joe the Driver jumped out and waved down Dennett. He escorted the great man over to my door and opened it wide. Dan Dennett, meet James Plath.

Well hello, boomed Dan.

Hey there, I said.

A limo? Dennett asked.

Sure, after all, you are Daniel Dennett! You deserve it! Jump in, Dan, I said.

So, I'm sitting across from one of my favorite philosophers. What do I say?

Want some wine, Dan Dennett?

Wine?! Dan asked excitedly, smiling.

I warned him that this stuff wasn't anything too fancy, but I bought it because the greatest guitarist in the world drinks it, so I thought I'd try it, it's a cabernet. Eddie Van Halen loves it, I said.

Hey, Dan, we're having a cab inside of a limo, I quipped.

Ha! Well, if it's good enough for Eddie, it's good enough for me, boomed Daniel Dennett.

So Dan and I had a few bottles of wine and a very pleasant trip back to Long Island, New York. I had secretly told Joe to take his time on the drive, to make it last. Joe winked and said of course. After all it was a stretch limo, I had told Joe. Let's try and stretch time!

Dan and I had a great talk. We discussed many topics, ranging from consciousness to jazz to skepticism, from Randi to Hofstadter, and of course little things like the meaning of life and death.

Light stuff.

For Dan, consciousness was obviously a result of neural circuitry and when the brain died, so did its consciousness. I totally agreed. How could there be a soul? Impossible. Dan said if there was a soul it was made out billions of tiny robots called neurons. The mind was merely what the brain does. I agreed.

The celebrated author of the great book *Consciousness Explained* and I toasted to our finitude on that rainy day in The Milky Way.

THE AMAZING RANDI

Dan told me what a fan he was of Randi's and I told him all about me studying with Randi and what a life changing experience it has been and gave him a few good Randi stories.

Dan just loved the story about a reporter who was interviewing Randi on the topic of psychics. They sat at Randi's dining table and at one point Randi asked the reporter to make a drawing of anything he wanted. Randi turned his back. The reporter was directed to seal the secret drawing in an opaque envelope. Then to seal that envelope inside another opaque envelope. The reporter did so and then Randi turned back around and the interview went on. Great questions were asked and even greater answers were given by Randi.

At one point the reporter accidentally spilled his coffee. He made quite a mess and apologized a lot. Randi told him it was no problem and had it cleaned up in no time. The interview went on for another half hour or so.

The reporter then asked about his drawing. Would Randi like to try and discern the hidden contents?

Randi said okay, he'd give it a try. He held the envelope to his forehead. Closed his eyes. Concentrated. Randi's eyes soon opened and he grabbed a pen and pad. He started sketching something, warning the reporter not to say a word and Randi was saying it's probably wrong, but...

He held up the drawing for inspection.

The reporter looked on in amazement. Randi had done it! The reporter tore open his envelope. And then the first envelope. When he pulled out his own drawing and held it next to the drawing Randi had just made, the drawings matched! Exactly!

The reporter left in amazement.

But how did Randi do it?

Randi told me exactly how he had hoodwinked him. It was Randi himself who had "made" the guy spill the coffee! It looked so accidental that the reporter himself thought he had caused it. During the clean up, Randi had stolen the envelopes with the drawing inside under the cover of some paper towels and napkins. Once in the kitchen, Randi opened the envelopes and caught sight of the drawing and then resealed it again in two new matching envelopes.

Then he slipped it back out into the dining room under more paper towel coverage and put it right back on the table while the reporter was still busily wiping up the mess and feeling sheepish. It was then only a matter of Randi waiting for the reporter to ask him to try the trick and then divining the contents of the envelope. Pretty amazing...

Dennett roared!

Finally, Joe said we'd arrived at the Three Village Inn where Dennett would be staying. We said goodbye and Dan said he was looking forward to seeing some of my own magic in the morning when we'd have our meeting on Darwin Day.

Sure. No pressure.

No sleep, either!

DARWIN DAY!

The next day I woke up after an hour of sleep and it was Darwin Day. I was to meet with Dennett and a few of my friends in my office. The thing was, I didn't have an office. See, everyone on the itinerary had a PhD and an office on campus. Now I was no slouch in the degree department. I was just finishing up my third master's degree at the time, but didn't have an office on campus, so I put in a call to the Honors College there where I was an alumni and asked if they could help me out.

They were so nice and completely understood my predicament. They did a little searching and called me right back letting me know that the honors conference room was now officially, for Darwin Day, James Plath's office! They even put my name on the door. How cool is that?

My two good friends Chris and Bill joined me that morning and together we bought piles of donuts and rolls and delicious bagels and some coffees and we rearranged the furniture and set up the room just right. It didn't hurt that Chris was an architect and that Bill built houses. They knew their stuff! Both were also big skeptics and Daniel Dennett fans, so I figured it would be nice to share this day with them.

Well, we had a blast.

Bill was pretty calm throughout it all, but Chris was nervous. This was the first time I had ever seen Chris nervous. That goes to show you what a big deal Dan Dennett is. We were all excited to talk to him. Soon I told them that I heard footsteps coming down the hall.

Here comes Mr. Dennett.

Of course we had an incredible meeting with the great man and yes, I did perform some magic for him. Dan then signed my copy of the book he had co-authored with Douglas Hofstadter called *The Mind's I.* He wrote:

Dear James,

To a real magician from an amateur magician.

Your friend, Dan Dennett

Later, Dan invited us to see a private lecture of his that was only for the philosophy and physics departments. He shared brilliant insights into the nature of consciousness. That night after dinner he gave a mind bending lecture on free will for the public.

We were front row. It was sold out. What an amazing two days!

Ever since Darwin Day, if I ever had a major philosophical question or some dilemma had me baffled, I'd write Dan and he would always, without fail, fire back a helpful and satisfying answer. He is a wonderful guy and I'm honored to call him my friend.

SIMON SAYS

There was one more philosopher that I would often keep tabs on, googling him every now and then to see what he was writing. He is the author of the book *Very Little, Almost Nothing: Death, Philosophy, and Literature*, his name is Simon Critchley, and he taught in England. That book I just mentioned blew my doors off! It was such a well written and great book on death and atheism, filled with Friedrich Nietzsche and Samuel Beckett and other giants of literature and philosophy. One day I googled Simon and to my surprise learned that he was here in the states. In New York City! Living here and teaching at The New School for Social Research.

I fired off an email telling him what that book did to me and asked if I could drop by and meet the man. Simon graciously wrote me back and said sure and we set up a meeting. We talked for hours, mainly about death and dying. We were both obsessed with mortality. Simon said he was in the process of writing a book, something about graveyards and how people die. I told him that *Very Little, Almost Nothing* had rocked me just as much as Ernest Becker's books had. Simon didn't know Becker's work, so I filled him in on the great book by Becker titled *The Denial of Death*. If you ever get a chance, read this book. Powerful stuff!

Ernest Becker won the Pulitzer prize for this great book and then sadly died of cancer the very next year. Whew. So it goes.

That day in Simon's office was the start of a very warm friendship. Simon's book about graveyards turned into *The Book of Dead Philosophers*, a book about how great minds approach death and dying and details how incredible philosophers died. Get it, you'll love it. He even thanked me in it.

To promote it, Simon's friend, the stunning Brooke Geahan, threw a book party that only she could arrange, star-studded with authors and actors and all sorts of interesting and beautiful people. Simon asked me to do a mock seance during it, seemingly contacting the dead philosophers and conjuring up some mentalism to entertain the crowd.

All I can say is it was a wild night of philosophy and magic and wine and mayhem (I won't even *mention* the playboy playmate and the kissing contest) and later Simon and his beautiful wife, the psychoanalyst Jamieson Webster offered to let me crash at their place in Brooklyn and once again there I was, The Skeptic's Apprentice, being tucked in by one of my heroes. Amazing.

Simon and I bonded on a similar theme. Death. We were both fascinated and tormented by this idea of finitude, the final ending, Shakespeare's undiscovered country that no one returned from. Simon and the author Tom McCarthy even have a group called The Necronautical Society, where they write about and study death. They both loved my magic and so they made me The Necronautical Society's honorary magician. You can't make this stuff up, folks. But wait until later, when I tell you what the great Simon Critchley is up to nowadays. Astonishing!

Now, let us get to the core of this book.

Let's get down to business, shall we?

Yes, this is it. The table has been set. Here we go. Please give this your full attention. We have now arrived at the most interesting and at the same time most secret part of our journey.

Ladies and gentlemen, I now give you, the mystery of all mysteries.

TRUE ASTONISHMENT

One day, not too long after meeting Raymond, sometime in 2008, I walked into Ronjo's Magic Shop and there, sitting on top of Ron's desk was a magic magazine and on the cover was, yep, you guessed it, Paul

Harris. He looked just like a monk. Shaved head, wearing a hoodie, sitting in the woods, looking into the camera, looking right through me. He still had that trademark mustache.

There was a full interview with him, the first one in many years.

Immediately I begged Ron (who by this time had become my very close friend), I pleaded, I had to have this magazine. I'd pay anything, but I just could not leave without it.

How about free, Ron said happily.

Free? I was beaming. I took it home and slowly devoured the new interview. Paul was indeed living everywhere. Parks, benches, he even lived in a teepee for a time. The interview quoted him saying that he was a child of the world and that everywhere was home. I loved that. The interview also announced that Paul would be releasing a brand new box set called True Astonishments. A nine DVD set of new magic ideas. Jesus Christ. Nine! What more could I ask for?

Wait...there was more!

The kicker was that the first three hundred people who purchased the set through his website would get the box signed by Paul Harris himself and would also receive permission to enter an exclusive private group forum chat with Paul on the internet. A live chat. With Paul Harris. Here was our chance to reconnect!

I quickly found out who was running the chat. It was someone named Jason and so I wrote Jason a message and introduced myself. Well, Jason turned out to be a great guy and we quickly became email friends. I told Jason my story about meeting Paul way back at Ronjo's Magic Shop and I told him about the address Paul had given me and about his house burning down.

I also mentioned that I was Randi's apprentice. Somehow Douglas Hofstadter's name came up and it turned out that Jason was a big fan of Hofstadter's work and together we shared ideas and discussed Doug's books on consciousness and then I took a shot and gave Jason my phone number and told him I'd really appreciate it if he could pass it or my email on to Paul with a little message.

The message read:

Dear Paul,

Have realized for sure that the idea of a "self" or an "I" is a myth, a fiction. There is no self. Have a feeling there's more to this mystery of consciousness. Would love to talk again.

-James Plath, The Amazing Randi's apprentice.

PS- We met years ago at Ronjo's Magic Shop in New York and later talked philosophy late into the night.

PPS-You owe me a pork chop.

CHATTING WITH PAUL

The box set arrived and it was beautiful and chock full of magic ideas that only Paul Harris could conjure up. He had done it again! Then the day of the chat arrived but sadly, there was no word from Paul Harris at all. But that was okay with me. This guy had given me so much joy through his books, so much magic, so much happiness over the years, I couldn't expect anything more. The Q and A chat was very interesting and it lasted for like three or four hours. I even managed to get a few questions in, which was no easy feat with so many people clamoring to discuss magic ideas with Paul. Paul actually answered all of my questions. It felt really nice to connect for a bit, even though it was in this busy forum with so many fans trying to get his attention and talk about magic.

Throughout the entire chat there were tech problems and what happened was we couldn't see Paul at all. We could see Jason, who was in a different location than Paul, and what Jason wound up doing was calling Paul from his cell phone and putting him on speaker-phone and holding the phone up to the camera so we could all hear Paul.

A few times Jason held the phone in such a way that I could almost see Paul's phone number flash by on the screen. I made out a digit here and a digit there and quickly jotted them down, all pieces of a puzzle leading to maybe once again connecting with my hero!

But, alas, Jason must have realized he was accidently flashing Paul's number and he quickly turned his hand down so it was only the back of the phone showing for the remainder of the chat.

Foiled again!

After about four hours or so the chat wound down and Paul said goodbye to us. We all thanked him so much for such a priceless treat.

My little beagle, Eugene (named after the French absurdist play-wright Eugene Ionesco!) was just begging to go outside in the yard and do that absurd thing us animals are forced to do with our plumbing. So, a little sadly I must admit, I shut down the laptop and took Eugene out into the backyard to do his thing. Out there under the stars and that moon I was grateful to have been able to reconnect briefly with Paul Harris and dreamt of a time maybe in the future when I would be able to somehow, someway get in touch with him again and discuss philosophy and consciousness.

I came back inside a few minutes later and noticed a missed call on my iPhone. It was an unknown number, looked to me like a California or Florida number. Probably a telemarketer.

Or...could it be?

I dialed it and held my breath. The phone rang two times and then I heard the most welcoming voice on the other end say, Hi, James.

I said hello...

The voice on the other end of the phone said, Hey, it's Paul.

And so it began.

Again.

The Only Game in Town

What a talk that first phone conversation was! We talked for hours and hours about Randi, about skepticism, and mainly we talked about consciousness. We agreed on the idea of no self. The Buddhists called this non atman. Atman meant self. It was great to hear that Paul also didn't believe in the notion of a self and we discussed thinking and we discussed thinking about thinking (!) and the whole wild mystery of consciousness.

Paul said that consciousness and philosophy of mind was the only game in town. I wholeheartedly agreed. At one point Paul asked if I had thought much about perception and had I ever wondered about the idea of perception's knobs being twiddled with.

Could we tweak our perception? Was the reality we were perceiving right now ultimate reality?

I admitted I hadn't given that much thought, but that it made sense.

What if what we think of as reality isn't really it? Paul asked.

You mean, like cleansing the doors of perception, I said, throwing some Blake and Huxley at him.

Ah, Blake. Exactly, Paul said. Have you ever read Huxley's book on this? *The Doors of Perception?*

I smiled. I just knew he'd know! And he had gotten *both* references.

No, I haven't read it yet, but I do own it. I told him I had read Huxley's masterpiece, *A Brave New World* (given to me for my birthday by my good friend Paulina) and that I had loved it. Paul suggested that I read *The Doors of Perception* and then he gave me some other things to investigate, including the philosophy of some guy I'd never heard of, the anthropologist Terence McKenna. I wrote down all of his suggestions and kindly thanked him and said goodbye and just hoped we would talk again sometime.

Back in the Saddle

Little did I know that Paul would call every day, for years.

Every day.

One day, early on in our friendship, I was on the phone with my Mom and we were discussing a paper I was about to write for school and the other line beeped through and I saw who it was and told her that it was Paul Harris, but I'll just have to call him later. I really had to get going on writing this paper. My mom laughed and said with great gusto and amusement, Jim, did you ever think that the day would come when Paul Harris would *bother* you?

We both laughed. It was such tremendous a gift to be able to talk to one of my all-time heroes *any time* I wanted to and to discuss the only subject I wanted to discuss - consciousness!

It truly was astonishing. And still is.

THE DOORS OF PERCEPTION

So I started looking into all of Paul's suggestions. I looked up this Terence McKenna person that Paul had recommended and at once I just knew that I loved the guy. What a great mind and what a wonderful way of writing and speaking, Terence was a real character! If you don't know of him and his work, please do look him up and read him or just listen to a talk of his online. A big part of McKenna's message is his warning us about the dangers of culture and how culture *is not your friend* and how we must transcend culture in order to find our true selves. He discusses consciousness and the effects psychedelics produce on consciousness, just as Huxley had done. McKenna is entertaining and insightful and makes wonderful analogies along the way, such as comparing the study of physics and matter to the study of consciousness and how to understand matter we accelerate and smash particles into one another and then look at the pieces and what comes out of the collision and so if we are to understand consciousness we can take a psychedelic and this bangs things around and shakes up and careens things about in your cranium in order to understand the inner workings of the mind.

I picked up my copy of *The Doors of Perception* and read it in a couple of hours. I'll tell you, once I picked this book up, I could not put it down. It was riveting! Huxley wrote about taking a psychedelic called mescaline and looking at all of these flowers and at art and describing the changes it had on his perception. He saw the answers to the tremendous mystery of existence that day on mescaline and he wrote about it all so beautifully and lucidly.

Maybe everyday perception and our senses weren't giving us the truth after all!

The very next day I went to the bookstore and grabbed a big stack of Zen and Buddhist books on the mind and start reading them in the café, along with more of the great Terence McKenna. I was reading up a storm. I also emailed Paul right there from the table and told him how much I was enjoying reading all these great ideas, but in a new light.

Paul warned me not to get too caught up in words.

But to me, words were all we had.

Paul told me that Terence called spoken language *small mouth noises*. Paul said words pointed to the truth, but we're just pointers, not the true thing.

So I sent an email of just a dot back to him.

" . "

He replied with an email of his own, only it was blank. I guess he won that round!

∞∞

The brain is wider than the sky
For, put them side by side,
The one the other will include
With ease, and you beside.

-EMILY DICKINSON

THE PURE WHITE LIGHT

That night during our talk, I told Paul that I thought he was right about twiddling the knobs of perception and that maybe this thing we call "reality" we see and experience all around us all the time isn't the only reality or maybe it isn't even the right one.

If there even was a right one!

I told him that I wanted to deepen my perception. To broaden it.

Paul said that he knew then and there that he was right about me. That I had a spacious mind.

One day Paul asked me to think back to my very first encounter with magic and astonishment. I told him it was when I watched a magician on television float a beautiful lady in midair. Man, it just took my breath away!

For Paul, it was when his uncle magically smashed a newspaper-covered glass right through a table top. He was hooked!

It was a moment of ecstatic bliss where every thought was pulled from his face leaving nothing more than empty space. I told him I had felt the same way. Just jaw-dropping, pure white light astonishment. We both agreed that after experiencing that, we knew we had to experience moments like it again and again.

Paul then asked me if I had ever heard adults compare themselves to children after seeing my magic. I told him, yes, that I got that all the time.

Even the brilliant Douglas Hofstadter had told me this:

I am incredibly impressed by your amazing artistry. I really almost never have the foggiest idea what is going on when you do your tricks. And mostly, I don't want to know -- I just love experiencing the sensation of utter mystery, almost in the same amazed, goggle-eyed way as a child must experience a magic trick.

A CHILD-LIKE MIND

Paul explained what Douglas Hofstadter and others were trying to say, was that for a brief moment they had experienced a clear primal state of mind, they associated with a child's state of mind. Somehow the adult experience of astonishment triggered this feeling of what it felt like to be a child. Paul likened it to the same experience that seduced both of us into performing magic in the first place. That jaw dropping, pure white light moment of astonishment. He said that if you follow those footprints, it takes you right up to the crumbling edge of everything we think we are and just beyond to a state of mind we experienced naturally as small children, but society devalued and then made taboo as we became adults.

BLANK SLATES AND MIND BOXES

When you come into the world, you enter it as a blank slate, or a tabula rasa, as the great empirical philosopher John Locke put it. You don't have any ideas about who you are or what anything is. You're just pure being and this feels great because there are no options, or opinions, or judgments. There is no right or wrong. Everything is everything. That's what you see in a baby's eyes.

Pure child's mind. Wholeness.

Paul went on, saying that soon, very quickly, we learn stuff. We learn the names of ten thousand things, who we are, what we're supposed to be, and what's good and bad according to the current rules of the game. We label everything. And we organize all of this information into little boxes.

Kant! I shouted.

Can, Paul said, smiling. It's true.

No, Kant! Immanuel Kant, I said. The philosopher. He said the mind was like a post office, it was constantly filing things in little boxes.

There you go, Paul said. You just put all of what I just said into the little box named Kant.

Paul went on explaining that when any new information comes along you file it into the appropriate box. Right now you might be filing these thoughts into your Immanuel Kant ideas box. I understand. You're just doing your job. You've been trained to do this since birth. You have thus created your world view. There's no particular reality to any of this. But it's in your head and you know the territory and it's where all of your thoughts do their thinking.

But we quickly forget what was there in the first place, because these thousands of little thought-boxes are stacked up so tight that the original clear space of child's mind is completely covered up.

It isn't gone. It's just blocked by this wall of overstuffed boxes.

Eclipsed! I said. Like a veil!

Exactly, Paul replied. Then along comes something strange, like a clever magic effect. Let's say this book vanishes from your hands. Poof, no book. Your trained mind races into action and tries to put a strange event into one of its rational boxes. But no box will hold it. At that moment of trying to box the unboxable your world view breaks up. The boxes are gone.

What's left? I asked.

Ah, said Paul, smiling.

Simply, what was always there, your natural state of mind.

That's the moment of astonishment.

The sudden experience of going from boxes to no boxes. If you can keep the fear response from arising you have the experience of going from a cluttered adult mind to the original clear space. Gee, it almost makes you feel like a kid again.

So that's why Doug had said my magic had reduced him to an amazed goggled- eyed child. Wow!

There it is, said Paul. Now for most people, the moment lasts less than ten seconds. Then because we crave the security of our missing world view, we quickly build a new box.

The "it went up your sleeve" box or the "it was all done with mirrors" box or even the "I don't know what happened but it was all a trick" box. And that's all it takes. One thought, one guess, even a wrong one and the boxes all come back and the natural mind gets covered up (veiled!) and the moment of astonishment is over.

Astonishment is Your Natural State of Mind
Astonishment is not an emotion that's created.

Astonishment is an existing state that's revealed.

Paul said that if you learn to surrender to the moment, let it sink into the astonishment, you will be rewarded with a deeper more sustained experience. But, if you fight the moment or treat it like a puzzle to be figured out, you will get what you paid for, non-astonishment.

The astonishment is real.

It's not the same as the trick. The trick is the tool. The astonishment is a brief flash of our natural state of mind. A place we should all experience more often. The magic tricks are helpful tools to help unleash the moment. In a nutshell, Paul said, you're using magical illusions to dissolve cultural illusions in order to experience a moment of something real.

Whew. Astonishment is real. Surfing at the center of the big gasp is at the heart of magic. Not only did this change the way I approached my magic but I could see where Paul was heading.

Paul was saying that I had to meditate and use meditation as a tool and to get into that state without the magic, just by stopping my mind, stopping the chatter. Little did I know that this was just part of something much bigger. How could I have any idea that what he had in store for me was much more than that?

The whole enchilada. The whole shebang! Little did I know that Paul Harris, my hero, was about to lay some very heavy philosophy on me. That he was about to introduce me to what is called the mysterium tremendum and that he was about to share with me something I had been searching for for many years.

Paul Harris was about to share with me the true meaning of life.

Dream Dialogue
Three

❧

Me: Randi, what if all of this, this whole world and everything and everyone in it, is really just some strange dream?

Randi: Well, it's possible. Certainly possible. People have said that very same thing for thousands of years...

Me: But, what if...

Randi: Thousands of years, Jimmy. But, there's a problem. It can't be verified.

Me: Well, what if I told you that it CAN be verified?

Randi: (drums his fingers along his cane)

Me: All you need to do is look into the telescope.

Randi: (reaches for the cane)

Me: Hold on, hold on!

Randi: (eyes twinkling) Okay, okay. Proceed...

Me: The way to know if you're dreaming or not is to wake up.

Randi: I suppose...

Me: So, the way to verify that this is a dream is for us to wake up...

Randi: Yes, but how?

Me: Ah, glad you asked. First, one must stop all thought. Silence the mind. This can be accomplished by meditation. Total silence. Totally in the present moment, the only moment, and to realize, truly realize, that there is no self.

Randi: (eyebrow raised) Go on...

Me: In total silence, where the constant chatter of the monkey mind is ceased, something happens! A shift occurs! One of paradigmatic proportions! The illusory self is dropped and suddenly you realize your true nature.

Randi: Which is?

Me: Everything! You become one with everything and a beautiful peace comes over you.

Or rather, you come to the realization that what you truly are IS that very peace.

You are love. Infinite consciousness is your true nature and you realize that this world that we're existing in is merely maya, merely your dream. Whew!

Randi: (tapping his cane in his hand, but listening intently, begins to hum *Row Your Boat* under his breath)

Me: (smiling) Exactly! Merrily, merrily, merrily, merrily...

Randi: (sings softly) Life is but a dream...

CHAPTER 3

A Hard Pill to Swallow

∾

Our claim to own our bodies and our world is our catastrophe...

-WH A*UDEN*

PRE BIG BANG

TO EMBRACE THE BODY AND the world is to embrace the idea of death. Paul often urged me to think about myself before I was born. Better yet, to think of the universe before it came to be. It's a very fine thing to ponder, to go *pre big bang*. Great thing to bring up at parties. Try it. Ponder for yourself the situation of vast endless infinite empty space and try to answer the question of how out of this empty endless void *anything at all* was created. I would think of this all the time. Out of nothingness, or somehow *compressed* nothingness, came everything.

Something tricky was going on here. Something was up. Like the Buddha had said in his wonderful Heart Sutra, form is emptiness and emptiness is form. Form is really compacted emptiness and emptiness is thinned out form.

I told Paul my thoughts on this and how I was thinking that maybe it was that the universe *in* the head was like the universe *outside* of the head and that thoughts flow and all of these complex processes occur, but the "self" gets in the way and takes credit for it all and locks "you" seemingly *within* when really everything was all just one.

I felt like I was just starting to grasp all of this intellectually, but it was still extremely hard to believe. It was just so damn counterintuitive. But, I didn't give up.

I knew that the real thing to ponder here was how can any of this possibly be real? What the heck is really going on here? What is this endless emptiness and where did it come from? If you feel the same way, my dear reader, stay with it and don't flinch and it will eventually short circuit the chatter pretty quickly and just leave you basting in the infinite astonishment of it all.

Are you feeling it?

You will.

You wait and see!

A Hard Swallow

Then one fine day Paul hit me with the most astonishing thing I've ever heard in all my life. Buckle up, because I'm about to share this with you and it is the core message of this book.

He said that actually, and this is a really hard swallow, that this world is made out of the same stuff as dreams. Imagine having a lucid dream, where you are aware that you are dreaming. All the "very real" things in the dream are going on while at the same time there is an awareness that the entire dream is simply a projection of pure imagination.

You are that pure imagination that becomes aware of the dreaming.

Your head, your brain, your body are all part of the dream. This becomes completely obvious when "you" finally see it.

It seems impossible until you do.

That's why this thing is called the mysterium tremendum. That pure imagination is the transcendental object at the end of history; it is the attraction of this endless imagination slowly becoming aware of its own imaginings. At the moment of full awareness it recognizes that it is the dreamer of the dream and thus wakes up. Thus ends the dream of history (the dream of a world and bodies) with the one endless mind knowing its own infinite perfection.

❧

Every man takes the limits of his own field of vision
for the limits of the world.

-ARTHUR SCHOPENHAUER

LIMITLESS

Well, needless to say, that night I couldn't get much sleep. How could I? My world had been turned inside out! Could this whole thing really be a dream? No wonder the physicists couldn't find matter! No wonder the psychologists couldn't find consciousness! Maybe truly there wasn't a bottom to it all.

My next talk with Paul was riveting. Paul was now honing in on it all. He wasn't holding back. We discussed the nature of the dream, the nothingness, and the void. We pondered death and the concept of no self and the idea of eternal emptiness.

I had read about and thought about all of these subjects before, but now they were taking on an entire new level of understanding. I also loved every word. After all, this was the kind of stuff I lived for. Now Paul Harris was showing me that this was the true meaning of Zen, of Buddhism, of Taoism, that this was the true meaning of life itself:

To wake up from the dream of existence.

Of course, being a serious skeptic, I had to ask how I can know this for sure.

Ah, the way to know if it is a dream is simply to wake up, Paul said.

So this was enlightenment! No wonder Buddha's name literally meant the awakened one. Enlightenment was called an awakening. It was a transcending of dualism. I knew all this but had missed it somehow.

I had read hundreds and hundreds of books on Buddhism and Zen and I still missed this! What had happened was my mind was programmed to take in knowledge and to fit that knowledge into the scope of my world view. We see things based on the particular paradigms we are locked into at the time and we only let in what agrees with that viewpoint.

I had thought that I really understood and knew the concept of no-self, but apparently I had only *barely* understood it intellectually. I had totally missed this notion of an awakened state, a stateless state where there was no thought, wherein we apparently find out who and what we truly are, with all of this occurring only in the present moment.

Missed it!

I had always taken the idea of being in the present moment to mean don't miss the precious present because you are thinking about the past or anticipating the future. I had no idea that there existed a no-state state that occurred only when one truly stayed in the present moment. I had no idea that this is when the idea of a self would completely vanish.

Suddenly, in a flash, I understood the importance of meditation. I understood how crucial it was to sit quietly in stillness and to silently let go of everything.

But yet, I only understood this in words, only intellectually. I was still looking at the finger, like an imbecile, and missing the moon, missing the truth I so craved.

THE MOON!?

I told my great friend Richard, who was also a philosophy major, all that I'd learned over the last month or so. Expectedly he was very resistant to any idea that this life we are living was all just a dream. He listened attentively, but kept telling me that he had just watched an amazing show on television about whales and was I actually saying that those great giant whales *were not real?* He was baffled.

What about the moon?! he cried out. He just couldn't believe his ears. With great patience, I explained to him that even *his brain* wasn't real. I said that it was only provisionally real, that it too was dreamt up! All of it is a dream.

Here I used the classic brain in the vat idea to illustrate the dream theory. I said that if your brain was in a vat, Richard, this body and brain right here in front of me wouldn't be real and that I, too, along with all the great whales and yes, even the spectacular moon, would all be part of pure imagination.

He tried very hard to understand this and he said he was going home to think about it all night. Then, just before leaving, he asked a great question.

He asked if he and I were having the same dream.

I said to think about what one of our favorite people the great Bill Hicks had once said, that all of life was a dream and that there is only one consciousness experiencing itself through all of us, subjectively. I told him to think of a crystal clear lake, where suddenly there is an appearance of a ripple. The ripple maintains its rippleness. The ripple is like the seemingly separate individual, the ego, the false self, but it is always really part of the lake as a whole.

It is never separate. There is only an illusion of separation.

It was a good talk and I could see how jolting this was for him. It was the same for me when I had first heard it. Richard went home to watch the film *The Matrix* and to ponder all of this new information. I had told him how I had started *The Matrix* once again the night Paul Harris had relayed all this dream stuff to me and it had blown me away more than ever with this newly attained knowledge of the dream.

The movie *The Matrix* was pointing at the very same truth. So was the movie *Inception*. And many more works of art and music. The message was similar.

Life was a dream and the meaning of it is to wake up.

As soon as I got home that night I sent Randi a short note laying out the idea of pure imagination and the dream scenario in detail. He replied in a more open minded way than I thought he would!

That sort of idea has been around a long time.

Interesting, but not amenable to testing or proof...

-Randi

Hey, at least he found it interesting!

I showed Randi's response to Paul and Paul's reply was *beyond* interesting:

Testing? 5 dried grams of magic mushrooms in silent darkness.

Remember, the way to prove you're having a dream is simply to wake up.

-Paul

Whew.

ON BRAINS AND RADIOS

As you might imagine, I had still had many questions. One of the biggest questions I had was concerning the connection between pure imagination, or pure consciousness, and biology. Don't forget, I was a strict card carrying skeptic and materialist. I had studied with the greatest skeptic of them all, James Randi. I had a BA in Psychology and was working on my fourth master's degree.

Yes, my fourth MA degree, this one in Experimental Psychology. The point being, I don't play around. This was serious business. I wore a neuron pendant around my neck, for Christ sake. I was hardcore and I wasn't just going to accept this on faith.

I had questions.

One thing that nagged at me was the following. Within the dream, wouldn't we have to admit that biology causes consciousness? Isn't that what everyone reputable is saying? Isn't that why a psychedelic like magic mushrooms or mdma would work in the first place, because psychedelics stir up the biology and that in turn would cause us to see differently?

Help me to understand what you mean, I asked Paul.

Paul explained that no one can prove this either way. The brain could be the "creator" of consciousness (which many think is unlikely) or it could be a receiver/transmitter/filter for endlessly existing consciousness. Just like to the uninformed, a radio could seem to be the "creator" of the music or it could be a transmitter/receiver of the music.

It's quite possible that the chemical action of the substance simply tunes the brain/radio to a certain frequency which allows it to receive/modify the forever existing consciousness. The chemicals act like little fingers that move the chemical dials on the brain/radio. Like chemically adjusting a telescope to get a clearer view of what's already out there in the cosmos.

My head was spinning now. Or was it? What head? Mind blown! Once again.

I quickly wrote Randi and asked his opinion on the radio analogy. I was sure he would say it was total bullshit.

And I was right.

Yes, I think it is wrong. He has "consciousness" existing independently of a brain. Wrong.

-Randi

Next, I fired off emails to the philosopher of mind Thomas Metzinger, who had just written a great book called *Being No One* and to my friend and the smartest guy in the whole world, Douglas Hofstadter. Hey, they didn't name a character Hofstadter on the television show *The Big Bang Theory* for nothing..!

Dr. Metzinger replied quickly:

The usual nonsense. The hardware of the radio is a metaphysically neces-sary condition for music to be heard. The event has a history, but what counts are the constitutive conditions, what determines its existence here and now. He hasn't understood the problem, and constructs a straw-man. Nobody says that "the music is created by the radio".

You just cannot do philosophy on that level of conceptual resolution.

-Thomas

Okay, so that was two for two for materialism. Hofstadter would make it three for three. Doug replied in pure Hofstadter fashion and in great detail:

To me, there are proofs galore that consciousness is a function of biologi-cal processes. When brains are operated on and specific areas are tam-pered with, all sorts of things happen to one's awareness, for example. If parts of the brain are removed, all sorts of effects take place.

About the radio analogy, well, our brains are of course invaded by memes from the outside, just as a radio is invaded by radio waves from the out-side -- but whereas the radio doesn't store the waves in itself permanently, our brains do store those memes (or some of them) permanently, and they become part of us. And "part of us" is very literal -- it means that those memes are incorporated into the physical structures of our brains.

Music is not composed by a radio but it certainly does come out of the radio's loudspeaker. In the same sense, what I say to you on the phone doesn't get dreamt up by your telephone, but it certainly is produced sonically by your telephone. In the case of brains, most of the stuff that a human brain makes happen (motor actions, speech, etc.) comes from inside it rather than outside it. In that sense, a brain is different from a radio or a phone.

But it's a bit closer to a CD player with a CD in it (or, for that matter, an iPod with lots of music loaded into it). In such a system, the music is all coming from the physical entity. Of course, the music still wasn't composed by the physical entity, but it is all coming from that entity.

Most people's ideas are not invented by them, but are just taken from the environment. Most people are not "idea composers" -- a great deal of what they say is simply copied from what other people have invented.

In that sense, most people are like iPod's filled with pre-recorded ideas that are ready to be triggered by external circumstances. Other people composed what they are going to say, and they merely say it when triggered.

Some people, of course, are much more original than this, and they compose new ideas. Their brains are also responsible for that, of course.

Over in doubt for now,

Doug

So Paul Harris' dream idea of nonduality was shot down by Richard, Randi, Metzinger, and Hofstadter.

And yet, I was still drawn to it. I just couldn't dismiss it that quickly.

Consciousness is *Prior!*

Paul sat down and read all of their replies with great interest and chuckled amusedly. He said that just as people assume matter is before consciousness, many people make a huge unproven assumption that biological processes create consciousness. There is absolutely no proof for this. And just as many smart folks will say consciousness creates biology. People confuse the mechanical descriptions of the brain and it's biology with its results, exactly like assuming that a detailed description of a radio and the electricity flowing through it proves that music is created by the radio.

This meant that Doug Hofstadter was still describing functions of the brain. You tamper with this part and this thing happens, you tamper with another part and something else happens. You could do the same thing with a radio and get all sorts of repeatable distortions of the music. It still doesn't prove that the music is produced by the radio or that consciousness resides inside the brain.

Another way to look at it is like a computer on the web. You push all sorts of buttons and get very specific results, but it's all just processing information that comes from someplace else.

And so it goes.

I had to admit, Paul did have a good argument. I could see it all more clearly now and it was making sense to me. If you ponder this and see how all this would work in a dream it helps.

Here we have the smartest guy in the dream showing me how tinkering with the brain proves consciousness is produced by the brain, but of course, me as the lucid dreamer would know better. And so would you. But we will get to that later!

Tinkering doesn't prove that it resides there, it only changes things, it doesn't show where it comes from. It's a tricky situation we are in. My own radio-head was spinning. Paul warned that I was *never* going to buy it intellectually, all I'd ever have is an experience and then it would be my call.

Remember, words point to truth. But aren't truth.

I needed direct experience! A life changing, direct experience.

I read everything I could get my hands on concerning life as a dream and the effects of direct experience through meditation or psychedelics on consciousness. Some great studies were done at Johns Hopkins University showing how psilocybin taken in a peaceful setting released terminal cancer patients from their intense fear of death through an abrupt change of consciousness. This now all made perfect sense to me. Like the radio or computer analogy, these people would know from direct experience that even when the radio or television set is broken the signal keeps right on broadcasting.

That is the whole game right there, to know this. Consciousness is prior to matter.

Again, consciousness is *prior* to matter. Know this.

Truly knowing this is what will transform this place.

Everything else is just folly.

❧

People are scared to empty their minds fearing that they will be engulfed by the void. What they don't realize is that their own mind is the void.

-Huang Po

The Ineffable

I quickly came to realize that the dream idea is a tough story to lay on people regardless of how open they might think they are or seem to be. It's just not a believable thing unless you wake up, just like with a normal dream. Even though our latest pure science tells the same story, it's a hard pill to swallow.

Reminds me of an old Zen saying:

Trying to understand from words is like washing a dirt clod in muddy water.

The beautiful thing in all this is it's the very best news possible about the nature of life. It means the best of you is forever in an ever growing state of expansive perfection.

A Very Brief Moment of Despair

One day I thought that I had upset Paul, maybe because I had said a few things that came off as annoying to him or maybe I just had one too many questions about such an ungraspable subject. He just seemed distant and not as fun.

Paul quickly sensed my worrying that I had bothered him in some way and wrote me:

I think what you may have felt is a moment of despair from me about the lack of practical tools and/or people's willingness to use them. I've read many versions of these words thousands of times.

I've shared many variations of these words with hundreds of people. Very little ever changes. I'm really not interested in philosophy or ideas or what smart people think may be going on.

I told him that I completely understood how he felt and that I was just trying to grasp it all by understanding other's ideas discussing the same thing.

Paul's reply had set me at ease. He said what we're interested in was *actual transformation*, not the words that point to it. It was a tough spot to be in.

He said that this situation occasionally inspired him to get out of the word business. He told me not to fret about it. Then he told me that I was doing great. All was well.

There just has to be a better way to activate people's higher selves than words. If words worked it would have happened by now. I thought it was astonishment for a while.

But it's only an experiential metaphor at best. I suspect that if this doesn't work we have to get out of the word game and do something completely different.

Dream Dialogue
Four

Me: (pointing at the window) Hey Randi, just look at that moon!

Randi: (looking up) Ah, beautiful, isn't it Jimmy?

Me: It sure is! And just as beautiful is the fact that you didn't look at my finger when I pointed at it, rather you looked at what I was *pointing at*, that beautiful moon.

Randi: Yes, yes, of course! Only an imbecile would stare at the finger!

Me: Exactly! Now, let's say that my finger represents words, concepts, and ideas. And the moon represents...

Randi: Truth?

Me: Yes! The point being, one shouldn't get hung up on the words and miss the Truth.

Randi: Very good, I like that. Sounds rather Eastern...

Me: It is Eastern!

Randi: Why do I have the feeling you're leading me into a discussion about dreams...

Me: Ha! You are correct, as usual. First I would like to share with you the names of just a few people who feel the same as me, that this life is merely a dream.

Not *like* a dream, but that it truly *is* a dream.

Randi: Well, let's see, the Buddha, for one...

Me: Yes! Buddha for sure. Also the Dalai Lama. Lao Tzu, the great Taoist. Oh! Speaking of Taoism, the author of the wonderful book *The Tao is Silent*, philosopher Raymond Smullyan, who, by the way, admires you very much, often writes about this life being a dream.

Randi: The man has excellent taste, I must say.

Me: (smiling) Speaking of taste, that reminds me...

I slowly reach outside the window and just pluck the moon from the sky and hold it in my hands before Randi's eyes and then I gently move it up to my mouth and I take a bite out of it, as if it were a juicy peach!

Randi: (just shakes his head and waves goodbye)

Randi wakes up alone in his bedroom. He peeks out of the window at the gorgeous moon in the sky and chuckles, dumbfounded.

CHAPTER 4

Down the Rabbit Hole

ARGUMENTS FROM AUTHORITIES

YES, I AM VERY AWARE that the title above is a fallacy. But for a moment, forget western logic. Try to think Eastern. Let us look at some of the amazing minds throughout the centuries that say the same thing that I have been saying about life being a dream. Maybe you know some of these names. Maybe you even admire a few of them. Maybe you admire all of them. Let us begin, shall we?

Buddha, Christ, Lao Tzu, Huang Po, DT Suzuki, Alan Watts, Jack Kerouac, Allen Ginsberg, Gary Snyder, John Cage, John Lennon, George Harrison, Eckhart Tolle, Meister Eckhart, Marguerite Porete, Thomas Merton, The Dalai Lama, Thich Nhat Hanh, Han Shan, all the mystics, all the Sufis, all the sages. That's just to name a few!

The search for self becomes the quest for no-self and this in turn becomes the search for True Self. Here is the analogy. Right now you are having a dream. Like dreams, your waking dream arises spontaneously. You, as the dreamer, dream up a character and this is your "self", your "I", your "ego". From the point of view of you as the dreamer, everything happens, or unfolds, and there is no control. Any ideas of control or free will are illusory.

In the dream, your dream character "self" has no free will, the dream is being dreamt by you, the dreamer, and that dream character is really just along for the ride. The dream character is a fiction making its way through life's dream. But from the point of view of the character within the dream, all appears to be real, even the notion of free will. But this isn't you, you are the dreamer.

This book is all about dissolving the imaginary blocks to your True Self.

How do you view life, dear reader? From the point of view of the dream or from the point of view of the dreamer?

RAMPING UP

I studied these ideas for a few years, discussing them with Paul daily by phone, through email, and through text messages. I meditated every night and after a while I really started to see the truth in it. This was the key to discover the meaning of it all. This was what all the sages were indeed pointing to. I watched every documentary and movie on it, read all the literature I could get my hands on, and studied meditation and the mystical and psychedelic experiences. Skeptically.

I was now seriously questioning the nature of matter. Questioning its apparent solidity. Questioning where it came from. Pondering the nature and architectural structure of a dream and constructing a conceptual map of awakening and toying with the idea of direct experience.

As you will do.

My meditation ramped up.

And then my beautiful and loving mother, who had been suffering from cancer for over a year, died peacefully in her bed in hospice.

I was now ready to embark on a journey into the unknown. The journey all true sages and contemplatives eventually make. The journey within, wherein I would ascertain the true meaning of the mysterium tremendum.

Thus began the journey from the light of reason to the source of all light.

Up in Smoke

Blowing smoke in Death's face, I took a long drag off my cigar and gently held my Shakespearian Hamlet skull up to my face. Soon *that* will be *me*, I thought. And sooner than later. Death is swift, be wise with your time. Now you see you, now you don't. Everything eventually goes up in wisps of smoke.

One night, one glorious night, I prepared to meditate as I had done every night for the past months. The preparation was very simple: lights out, in silent darkness. A sliver of milky moonlight peeked through the shades of my bedroom window, one of two rooms in my tiny, monk cell apartment.

The only sound in the room was the sound of my big heart beating. The heart that was broken permanently, first by the loss of my poor precious four legged canine best friend, Eugene, my beagle, dying and then by my sweet girlfriend of eight years flying the coop due to me not wanting to bring a baby into this just too big and often nasty mess of a world.

Fact: Armadillos nearly always give birth to identical quadruplets.

The last blow of all was the vanishing of my dear mother into the black endless void.

The Sufi poet Rumi said you must have your heart broken over and over and over again until it finally opens.

Nice words, but soon I'd understand exactly what he meant.

I could hear the sound of my poor finite heart, beating, the sound now faintly filling the room.

Slowly, ever so slowly, my heart decelerated. Softer, less rapid.

The heart of a blue whale is so big, a human can swim through its arteries.

A Loophole

Eyes closed, I began the silent journey within. Who knows? Maybe materialism was not the only way? Maybe there really was something else? Certainly not anything supernatural, paranormal, or occult. No laws of physics can be broken, this was for sure. But perhaps something else, something so essential, but just out of sight.

A loophole. Maybe!

Deeper and deeper into uncharted inward country traveled your new skeptical friend. As images and thoughts bubbled to the surface of my teeming consciousness, I told himself "not this, not that" and let them pass by like strange visitors in the night.

This old meditation technique of not this, not that, was used by the great sages and was called *neti neti*. If it worked for the great past masters, who was I to not use it? It meant when thoughts appeared in the stillness, allow yourself to dismiss them, by thinking "not this, not that."

Non attachment.

On this night it was working like a charm. The thoughts slowed, catching up to the heart, which seemed to have stopped. Seemed, but did not. The heart quietly and softly drummed on. A few more thoughts came and left and breathing slowed.

Silent Night, Holy Night

As thoughts, likes waves, began to slow, a peculiar thing occurred.

Any sense of a separate self, or an ego, or sense of "I" began to *gently dissolve.*

The "I" that *I* knew was a fake, a fraud, a farce, a myth, an illusion, now started to just melt away and a soothing wave of peace washed over what was left.

This sentence reminds you that this was one skeptical guy. Don't forget it!

Now, soaring deeper within, the ceaseless chatter of the always present cerebral calisthenics of monkey mind were totally halted and the sense of "I" was truly slipping away.

There are more fake flamingos in the world than real flamingos. Did you know that?

Shift Happens!

And then, just like that, *it happened*. What happened?

Something far beyond words. Something eff-ing ineffable. Something far beyond incredible!

The false sense of "I" gave way completely and my materialistic paradigm went *pop* and an extraordinary shift in perception occurred.

A flip of some inner switch, *click*, and suddenly I knew this was it.

I was IT.

Holy Shift.

I was, for lack of a better phrase, on the other side. The other side of *what?*

It was pure astonishment.

Here was the oneness the thousands of books I had read had discussed and here was the true meaning of Buddhism and Zen and Taoism and all of the religions. Here was what every sage spoke of when urging us to go within, here was the Nazarene's idea of the kingdom of heaven being within you, here was the Christ-mind, the Buddha-mind, the one mind of Huang Po.

Here was Nirvana. The extinction of the false self.

Out out, brief candle...

Unhoused At Last!

Out out, brief candle, life truly *was* a walking shadow. A poor condemned shadow ceaselessly shuffling in circles, hopelessly trapped in the hamster wheel of Plato's cave of the mind. On came a tremendous oceanic feeling, as if pure peace was washing over me. The true meaning of nothingness was finally understood.

Also, the genuine feeling of astonishment, my true nature. No "I", no "me", no "you", no mother, no father, no reader, no body. The experience was quite the thing.

But understand it is no *thing.*

Well, it is one thing, which is no thing, which is everything. Whew.

See? Words fail here. Pointless! Yet here I am doing my best to point it out to you. See that moon over there?

Whatever you do, don't get caught sucking on the finger that's doing the pointing, just discover for yourself what the finger is pointing at. Words will do that to you, they will comfort you and keep you in the dream. The finger is pointing out the way to see through this world and into beautiful never-ending nothingness. Since the night of my awakening, I now felt infinite and all encompassing.

It was as if a third eye had opened, but in my chest. My heart. I was everything. I was what we call god. I was what we call love. All was one. God truly is love. Not some being. Love *is* god.

Everything all made sense in an instant.

In a flash, here was the meaning of it all, tucked away deep inside, hidden and diligently guarded by this tenacious as a motherfucker sense of an "I" called the ego and protected by the most fantastic lie of all time, the lie that "you" are a person.

The truth is, *persons do not exist.*

"You" do not exist. And, there's nothing more real than nothing.

Really.

PARADIGM POPPER

Don't believe it? Believe me, I understand. Don't you worry, after you finish this book, you can see it for yourself. You'll try it. What do you have to lose? Besides your false personhood, your illusory "I". Your faulty view. Your worries of mortality. And everything else.

Go ahead. Pop your paradigm. Flip your perception inside out. While there's still time. Remember, the grave awaits. Lights out. Sooner than you think.

Vending machines are twice as likely to kill you as a shark is. Fact!

Back to the journey.

Remember how I said I could grasp it with words? Well, that's equivalent to eating the pictures of food on a menu.

The meal is what you want.

Or standing on a map and thinking you're in some new exotic location.

The map not the territory.

But now...

Here was the meal, here was the territory. No more menus, no more maps.

I was it.

Pure consciousness, pure awareness, one gorgeous, spectacular endless flowing of peace and love and knowing, oh *so much* knowing.

Knowing knowing knowing itself.

What a beautiful loop!

Such serenity, such brilliance, such joy. Here was the true infinity! Forget about the old idea of a monkey typing away forever and eventually arriving at the script of Shakespeare's Hamlet.

Here was a skeptical and upright monkey with a tail always bent towards finitude spinning a tale about his discovery of true infinity.

This was the mystical experience.

This sentence is going absolutely bananas right now!

By the way, a strawberry isn't a berry, but a banana is. Fact!

So are avocados and watermelon.

TIME AND SPACE

Time had totally stopped. I was outside of the temporal and spacial limits, I was limitless, had gone beyond belief, leapt beyond cosmogony!

A thousand seconds is just about 16 minutes. A million seconds is just about 11 days. A billion seconds is about 32 years and one trillion seconds is just about 32,000 years.

We think a trillion is a lot. But the good news is: Honey never spoils.

You can eat 32,000-year-old honey.

Sweet!

DEEPEN PERCEPTION

I wrote Paul immediately afterwards and told him what had happened.

"Welcome home" was his reply.

He told me it gets deeper and deeper to where it is obviously the true reality that the world and body illusion arise from.

At the very least I will find "myself" getting more and more peaceful, even if or when the outer world experience is falling apart.

All I knew was I wanted to deepen the perception of it. This was it, the true meaning of life. It was such a beautiful feeling and it was like a flip of a switch on reality, on what can be seen.

Huxley was right!

But I decided I wanted to go deeper into it because I was sure it would get even more beautiful, to the point of tears.

Meditation was the key. It was all a locked book until the key was found. It was astonishing, that open space communicating with its illusion of a separated self, just the one big endless mind trying to convince the sleeping dreaming part of itself to wake up from its dream. Eventually that space would become more and more my normal state and could be deepened with just a moment's pause.

So now my toes were in the wet sand of the beach and pointing toward the ocean. The real journey home had begun. Where you are going, dear reader, you won't need books or knowledge or a yoga mat or anything at all. Everything you need is already inside of you.

Let go of the dream.

I'm reminded of the great writer Joseph Conrad who felt that when a person is born they fall into a dream like a person who falls into the sea. It's all a matter of flipping the perspective, a matter of not valuing what you see all day in front of you.

The map is not the territory. The menu is not the meal. See? Sea? Si!

Dream Dialogue
Five

❦

Me: So you can't just tell me this is not a dream.

Randi: (grunts and groans)

Me: We are born into this. There is no easy way out. One must realize it's a dream by waking up.

Randi: Yes, but...

Randi wakes up in his bed! He simply cannot believe he was dreaming again! Scratches his head. Giggles to himself. Pinches himself. Laughs.

Randi: Astonishing...!

Randi sighs, then looks over to his nightstand. There, next to the lamp, sits the unfinished manuscript of this very book, The Skeptic's Apprentice!

Randi: Strange. Now why would *that* be here?

Oh...oh no...!

Randi wakes up AGAIN.

A double wake up!

Randi: Dammit! It all seems so real!

Randi glances slowly over at the nightstand. The manuscript is gone. He pinches himself. Giggles. Rolls over and goes back to sleep.

CHAPTER 5

Row, Row, Row Your Boat

❦

Talent hits a target no one else can hit;
Genius hits a target no one else can see.

-ARTHUR SCHOPENHAUER

EVERYTHING IS *WITHIN* YOU

IMAGINE THE SHIFT IN CONSCIOUSNESS when I realized that I didn't exist in a body? That a body existed *in me*? What a profound realization!

"I" no longer existed in the world. *The world existed in me.*

My whole life I just knew there couldn't be a soul hidden in the brain. I knew it.

But to realize it was really that *the brain was hidden in the soul?*

I wanted to shout it out over the rooftops of the world!

This book is my shout!

Many people can't admit that their philosophies of life might be wrong and I was one of these people. For a long time I just stayed locked in my comfortable paradigm of materialism and really believed that Randi and I had all the evidence on our side and that we were in the know.

Without a doubt.

Then I had this direct experience and learned the astonishing truth. What amazement! What surprise! No wonder Albert Einstein declared that the mystic emotion was the finest emotion one could hope to experience.

A Switch in Identity

It was earth-shattering to make the spectacular move from matter being first and making up everything in the universe to consciousness being first and foremost, consciousness being everything, to consciousness being the whole lot. When the shift occurs, any and all paradoxes fly out the window in an instant. Everything makes sense in a flash. For many years I had read tons of books, books on everything, I read anything good that I could get my hands on. But now I know the words aren't the truth. Some words point directly to the truth, but what you truly are all of the brainpower in the world cannot find. The intellect is caught up in fragmentation, in boundaries, limitations, and concepts, with all of this taking place in time and space, like those mind boxes Paul had pointed out.

This way of thinking, materialism, assures us that we're merely something that just transpired between the maternity ward and the boneyard. But really we are the *whole show,* the whole shebang! This has all been said innumerable times before by countless sages in voluminous volumes. The funny thing is, as I've said before, I read all of those books but still missed it, and maybe, just maybe, you missed it too.

Don't miss *these words*, my friend. The problem is that almost all of those books can be misinterpreted and taken as just poetry and the supreme communication gets lost. So let me be clear, I am not speaking poetical here, or just using metaphor. Everything I write here is true.

Twiddling the Knotty Knobs of the Doors of Perception

Wrestling with what had just happened and expanding meditation sessions to twice a day, every day, I had the sudden realization that the seeker was also a part of the dream. The quester was part of the illusion.

The path, the quest, must be dropped. You can't wake up, because *there is no you.* There's nothing to find. Absolutely nothing.

You, dear reader, are only a dream.

You. "You". *You.* There's absolutely no one to find.

You're already it.

True emptiness is even empty of emptiness. Whew. It truly is a jam packed void. The only thing that there is is nothingness which is imagining all of this.

The kicker is *that everything is You. Your dream.*

In fact, the book in your hands right now is a just dream.

These words? Dreams!

The word "word" is but a dream.

The word "dream" is a dream.

Dreamt up. Word up.

Wake up.

MORE HEAVENLY ADVICE

That sage named Jesus stated that the kingdom of heaven is within you. But what if there really never was any "you"? Well then, you *are* heaven. You are a heavenly dream. And all of this takes place within You.

See, all of these little dreamlike words have gathered here today to tell you that everything is alright, always. No matter what appears to be, it's really okay.

All is well. Believe it or not.

TO DIE BEFORE YOU DIE

To experience this directly, one must let go of things here. The less you desire, the more you gain of everything. Let go of it all. Drop it all.

It's all a dream.

This is why you picked up this book in the first place.

This is the answer to your question.

The question is also part of the dream.

The questioner is part of the dream.

The whole quest is part of the dream.

What you need to do is to simply wake up. Put the dream down. Right now.

Our purpose here is to dissolve the blocks to your True Self.

To show you how to die before you die.

Die to what?
To die to the idea of separation.
To die to the idea that you are your thoughts.
To die to the idea of identification with a body.
To die to the identification with an ego.
To die to the forgetting of who you truly are.
To die to your story of who you think you are.
To die to the idea of death itself.

And to remember. To remember that you already are free.

To die to any and all ideas and concepts and assumptions that you are not already free.

To die before you die.

The colossal question of existence can only be answered by realizing that there indeed is no answer. The quest can only be realized when one realizes this and stops questing and is very still.

Otherwise you search and search and never turn up anything. Simply be still. The dream of life absolutely abhors silence. It is in the noise business. It thrives on sound and fury and on chatter.

And motion!

Your only job is to stop all of that. Just this once.

Stop all thought and what happens is you wake up from total stillness as total stillness, as awareness. Pure awareness. Pure consciousness. Pure imagination.

You're swimming in it right now.

You *are* it.

Again, with Words...

Let me try and spell it out for you even clearer than that. This very real seeming world is just a dream. Not metaphorically, it's not just *like* a dream. It's not figuratively a dream.

It is a dream.

It is made of dream stuff. Pure imagination. Consciousness. It's totally imaginary.

Nothing is real here. Really.

Especially "you" and everyone you know or have ever dreamt of knowing. All of that is pure imagination. A wise man once told me that this pursuit of pure consciousness "is the only game in town." Man, was he right!

It's all a bubble. A mirage. A magic trick. Put it this way, this right here is the ONE trick that fooled James Randi! The trick of duality. Man, it sure is a good one. It fooled The Amazing Randi and you already know by now that you just *cannot* fool Randi.

Yet, fooled he was!

Devaluing the Dream

Right now, what you *are* is similar to a character in a dream you might have tonight wherein you dream of yourself, but in the dream you can't awaken. You think the dream is reality. What you *can be* is like a character in a dream that suddenly realizes the astonishing fact that it's all a dream and suddenly and lucidly wakes up within the dream. Aware.

Right now you're pulled in by the dream, you are taken by the dream, the pure imagination. You believe it to be real. How can it not be? Waking up, or enlightenment, is analogous to this dream character "you" stopping its caring about the dream. Letting go of the dream within the dream.

Devaluing the dream. Seeing through the dream. Becoming unattached. Eventually even seeing that seeing through the dream is all part of the dream! Then, dropping all thoughts and executing a Godelian or Hofstadterian leap out of the system.

While we're on the subject of things, ask yourself how there could ever be more than *one* thing? *Two* things? Impossible! There is only and there only ever was one thing. That one thing is pure imagination. Pure consciousness. Pure awareness.

And it isn't really a thing. Really, there is only no-thing.

Which happens to be everything. Whew.

The universal mind just wants company. Can you blame it? All alone for eternity. So, it imagines all of this. Dreams up this world, this entire universe. Imagines multiplicity. Imagines people and places. Pure imagination roams on and then gets caught up in its own imaginings.

Ah, therein lies the rub.

It believes the hallucination is real.

What about all the suffering in the world, you may ask? All of that pain? The truth is, it's all okay, always and forever.

Why? Because none of this is truly true. How could it be, if the whole world is not real, but merely a dream? The truth is that all of that pain is just a calling for home. A complex yearning for dissolution. A call to love.

What seems like a "you" and an "I" are but one and the same (no) thing fooling itself. The one supreme Self hallucinating all of this. We are mere imagination lost, we are imagination caught up in its own imaginations.

The truth of this is astonishing. Think of the ramifications! That would mean that everything truly is okay all ways and always and forever. No matter what! So smile, dear friend. You have absolutely nothing to worry about. Be absolutely fearless. There's nothing to be afraid of, ever.

Just like when you awaken within a dream at night, fear leaves you, because you know it's only a dream. Maybe a tiger was chewing on your leg for its dinner. Scary! But you wake up and you realize there wasn't really any tiger. Your leg is fine. You start dancing.

You're free because you *know* all is well. It was just a dream. That great poet sage Walt Whitman sure was right. To die is truly different from what anyone supposed.

And luckier!

DREAM DUST

Once you experience this shift in your identity, it's also astonishing how quick it is to shift back and once again be trapped in and involved in the dream. It's so easy to get snagged by it and forget the truth and get dream soot all over you! It swiftly covers up your True Self. The more you believe in the dream the more dream dust you'll have to dust off of yourself to get to the true You again.

This is where discipline comes in. It can take a while before the only thing you value is the True Self. Until then, you'll always be dealing with dream soot and fairy dust. This means more suffering. The trick is to practice being Being itself. Being itself is the true you.

You are Being, practicing at being Being itself!

Astonishing!

IT NEVER HAPPENED

Do you now see why all is always well?

Do you now see why I repeat this over and over again? To revisit it again, if all of life is a dream, well then it never really happened. If you spill milk, you might get upset. But if you are awake in a dream and you spill milk, you don't cry. You know it's just spilt dream milk on a dream floor or table. You know that when you wake up it's all clean. No mess. No floor. No suffering.

No crying over spilt dream cream.

When you awaken you will know that everything really is made of consciousness: You, me, the ground, the clouds, the sky, and yes, even THE MOON!

Everything is okay because it *already never happened.*

Right now I write now in the dream, righting the true nature of other dreamers who are reading me but are really me reminding myself to remember and not to forget the true reality of it all.

What?

Astonishment!

OUT OF OUR WORD REACH

Close your eyes. Stop your mind. See all of that blackness, all of that nothingness, no world, no particles, no nothing. Know nothing. Stay with that. Practice this meditation in silent stillness. Do it. What will you take away from doing this? Hopefully, in the end, nothing. Hopefully, if you're really lucky, *nothing will be attained.*

Finally! It's about time you got to truly know nothing. Intimately.

Right now, if you aren't meditating yet, these words might be confusing. The great writer and Buddhist Jack Kerouac once said of this remarkable enigmatic dream that *it was out of our word reach.* I like that. So true! To make another effort to put it plainly, you are here to transcend your circumstances and to remember your true identity. The only cure for existential despair is contemplation and the mystic experience. Period.

The mystic is the true genius.

Just imagine finding out that *you're already everything?* And you're nothing. All at once. Astonishing!

Everything is just at a different stage of the one pure consciousness. The difference between you and a chimpanzee is a matter of shades of that very same one consciousness. You and a bunny. You and a butterfly. You and cement! All pure consciousness, pure imagination...

THE CAT'S SILHOUETTE

It's all *one substance*, which isn't *really* a substance, but just pure imagination. It's all the Void imagining it's something rather than nothing. Like my little cat Shakespeare's silhouette cast on the bedroom window curtain, bathed in the moonlight, everything you see, everything you know, including what you take as your very own self, is merely a shadow cast by Universal Mind, a perched nothing, an objectification of the Schopenhauerian Will.

Your mission is to blast through this veil of illusion, leap beyond time and space, for only there is the one true holy ground, the groundless ground of no mind, of pure imagination. When this is accomplished, the final barrier having finally been pierced, the subject-object facade is forever smashed to metaphysical smithereens.

No subject, no object, no distinctions, no other, no-thing. Just You and your blissful radiance, which is only pure endless imagination. Don't avoid a void, dear reader. In other words, be your True Self and learn to truly be unavoidable! You *are* the Void, cleverly and hallucinogenically disguised as a person.

You will know this once and for all once you are (once again) the Void devoid of self. The answers to all of your questions are not *out there*, they are within. *Everything is within.*

You are not in the universe, but rather the true reality here is the universe *is within You.*

THE CERTAINTY PRINCIPLE

Let's try to eff the ineffable again. Ready? Here's the deal: I'm not in the world. The entire world is my idea. The whole wide world is within me.

Everything is within Me.

But not within my body. Or brain.

I am the whole space that everything rests in. Endless infinite space. Pure consciousness.

The trick is to out-Heisenberg yourself. To see yourself without you knowing you were looking! Catch yourself suddenly! Become aware of just who you truly are. Really.

A person, good or bad, is only a projection *in you*, the True Self, the one mind of pure consciousness. All people are all You: your parents are You, your neighbors are You, everyone is You. They are all a projection of the void. They are seemingly spaced out imagined people peopling imaginary space!

Yep.

This is the supreme reason why one shouldn't turn on others or be angry towards them. They simply don't exist as separate from your True

Self. It's *all* You, only it's You from another angle. A different perspective. A shift of point of view.

Direct experience illuminates this.

You need an ego with less width than that of Schopenhauer's thin coin to travel to the other side of that very same coin and to shift from what Kant called the phenomenal world to the only true thing, the noumenal. Pure imagination has dreamt up this idea of a "you" and pure imagination is not only within you, it *is* You.

Pry your True Self from the illusory false self known as "I". It isn't easy. But when it's finally seen, it sure seems like the simplest thing in the world. Behind everything is pure awareness driving the whole show, creating this entire dream. You're unaware of it, yet it is running beneath everything. It is why "things" *appear* to be here. Every part of what you call "you" is part of and made up of pure awareness.

This is why it can't be sidestepped or truly lost, because it's always there, only it is eclipsed by the tenacious ego.

Pure imagination is every "thing" and every "body" because every "thing" = one "thing" which is really a no-thing. It's all pure awareness, pure imagination, disguised as a thing.

Wholeness dressed up as stuff.

Got it? Are we having any fun yet?

The phenomenal world is all made up of pure awareness, pure imagination. These are merely words to you right now, but once "you" see it, all becomes as clear as a dew drop! The one no-thing makes up every seeming thing out of nothing.

The reality of the situation is that there is only nothing dreaming that it's something.

Which isn't!

I'm ready to do a backflip over here! How about you?

Pure awareness dreams and the entire universe bursts into being. From this vantage point, out there in space, we are all indeed star stuff, as Carl Sagan and Neil deGrasse Tyson so eloquently point out to us. But even deeper yet, *we are ghostly*, we are wonderfully fashioned nothingness in the shape of animals, plants, rocks, trees, seas, books. All is empty at the core of consciousness, empty and aware.

This shadow we call form or stuff or things just seems so real until we *truly see* for the first time, until we wake up and *realize* the truth with our *real eyes*.

What takes place is a tremendous shift, a paradigm shift from cognition to pure awareness. You must enact it. A rock can't do it, a rock cannot know its true nature. But we can, we can experience pure awareness through the portal of consciousness which is within us.

No wonder the wondrous Douglas Hofstadter loves self-reference. This is why!

We are pure awareness aware of itself!

At the dream level, the dream characters that are more aware of consciousness see through this strange dream of life. Most of the other characters don't see through the trickery and as a direct result they suffer more by not knowing what they are, a dream puppet.

If they only knew just who was pulling their strings. If they only knew this they'd laugh, for they would know the truth. They would realize beyond a shadow of a doubt that they are not this shadowy person they see before them, but really the dreamer underneath it all.

And that it's all okay, always and forever.

THE I-IDEA

Before we wrap up this chapter, think on this: every person has the very same i-dea of a sense of "I". It's true. They all think that they are this thing called "I", everyone even goes by the name "I", they refer to themselves as "I".

What does this tell us?

It tells us that "you" and "I" are everywhere and everyone and everything. All at once. There is only "I". Only You. Unbelievable right?

"I" know, trust me, "I" know.

But just wait until it happens to "you".

Until you meditate and experience this shift, you Kant know the thing in itself. The great Kant even went further than this, he declared that you Kant get to the noumenal while you're still alive. You Kant experience the thing in itself.

The good news is Schopenhauer showed us that you *Kan* get there. Schopenhauer, *along with every sage that ever existed*, gave to us the phenomenal secret, which is to die before death. A living death.

Die while you're still alive. Die to your false self. Die to your "I". Dissolve the false self and see your True Self.

Die before you die.

WHAT THE HELL IS PURE CONSCIOUSNESS?

Think on this: There are these two young fish swimming along and they happen to meet an older fish swimming the other way, who nods at them and says "Morning, kiddos. How's the water?"

The two young fish swim on for a bit, and then eventually one of them looks over at the other and asks *"What the hell is water?"*

What is this little story telling us?

Well, have you ever suspected something fishy is going on here in your life?

The answer to the riddle is this. Fish swim in the water, but they are unaware if it. It's what they *exist in*. It's *so close* that they Kant know it.

I ask you, what do you swim in, my friend?

It's my position that you swim in the great sea of being, but you are unaware of it.

Sea? See? We swim in the great ocean of Being.

We are really the sea, we are not the little wave. We just think we're the wave. We're convinced we are the wave. That's the ego. You're really the ocean.

You are just the Void wanting to know itself, to touch itself deeply, to become self-aware. Your answer to everything lies within. Answer the pull to being rather than the pull to desiring. Awaken from the dream of form and journey from the manifested to the unmanifested.

Pure awareness is dreaming the dream of manifestation. To suffer is to stay in the manifested, missing the unmanifested, and to remain lost in the dream of form, of separation, of individualization. Don't remain lost in the delusion of an illusion.

The object is not real, so how can the perception of it be real? Let alone the perceiver! It's all mirage, all manifestation, of no-things.

This sentence urges that when you get to the top of the mountain, to keep climbing...

Then, in a flash, desire suddenly flees and there is only complete contentment, a perpetual and perfect peace. Gone is sadness. Death can touch You not. This is true liberation.

Now I live everywhere and nowhere. For all is pure imagination. I live up on mountaintops and high in the stars. The very same stream pulsating through flowers, through sun beams, through rain, through you, blissfully courses through me. Eternally. It is only me now, but I am not lonely for I am everywhere and always, always in joy.

Dream Dialogue
Six

❦

Me: This world is made of dream stuff.

Randi: Ah, Shakespeare! We are such stuff that dreams are made on...

Me: No, really. It's all true. The very same stuff that makes up your dreams. Pure consciousness.

(Sprinkles some salt from the salt shaker into his hand and then onto the table)

Everything is that.

THIS. There's only this.

This is dream stuff. Its solidity is pure illusion. It's all consciousness.

Randi: (frowning) It just seems so real.

Me: Maybe you should salt your menu. It might taste a little better.

❦

CHAPTER 6

The Architecture of the Dream

❦

*I cannot be awake, for nothing looks to me as it did before, or else I
am awake for the first time, and all before has been a mean sleep.*

– WALT WHITMAN

THE PALACE OF NOWHERE

WELCOME TO CHUANG TZU'S PALACE of nowhere where all things are one.
Remove your shoes, pull up a seat and remember, no walking in anyone's head with your dirty feet. Let's begin.

If you find yourself having a bad feeling or a complaint, see this
as just a reminder that you've caught yourself sleeping. It's all dream,
so any complaints about a person or a circumstance is really all your
ego, all your dream, it shows that you are forgetting your true nature
entirely, which is wholeness.

When a conflict seems to arise, really it is just a dream situation
and once you know this in your bones it will bring you back to the noumenal even more. It will buffer it all and you will notice little or no
suffering, fear, or anxiety, only more and more freedom.

You will see that when you talk to others, you will connect not with
their egos, but rather with their true selves, which is really *your* True Self.
This is oneness. It's all a game of awareness seeking out and talking to
awareness. This will be the dawn of wisdom in your consciousness.

Think of all of this this way, it's all like a huge cosmic game of peeka-boo played on the grandest of stages.

You will notice an aching towards that inner portal to the True Self and when that pull back to the dream starts dragging you more and more back into the illusion you will notice it for what it is, which is the strange dream of existence, and you will notice the ever-present awareness within, the one constant, the pure consciousness.

Once you close this gap you will become very aware that all suffering or frustration is of the ego, the veil, the dream side of things and you will know for sure that the other side of the coin, the true side, is always there, always joyous, and the veil will be lifted.

We're all pointing the way for one another. As Jack Kerouac wrote, everyone is a bodhisattva. Those who are more aware point to the exit, the way out of the hallucination. The others who are less aware may point to the inside of the dream and keep you locked within it.

The idea is to be good to one another. To remind each other that everything is really okay. That all is well. To love one another as one and to love all creatures. Everything is beautiful when you don't believe in it. Unattach, before it's too late.

Soon you will learn to drop the dream like a hot potato and watch what happens when a character in the dream knows it's all truly a dream. What happens is you realize that *it's all You* and you know it's only your dream and then and only then does all suffering vanish.

You realize that there is truly nobody there to suffer!

When you are taken in by and believe in the dream, you suffer, because you are lost and are not your True Self. Instead, you're just some poor character, gone astray, far away from home. Waking up is the true end of all suffering for us walking shadows.

That is, of course, until you forget again.

Until you get caught in the dream again. Then there you go, you're once again lost, once again dreaming. Enter suffering, right on cue! There's a reason there's no place like home.

Because it's true.

If you can approach this with discipline and practice meditation as much as possible, you will be more and more joyful. The more you are aware, the more you are awake, and the less time you're snagged by the dream.

There's an old saying: First there are mountains. Then, there are no mountains. Then, there are mountains.

What this means is that first (before enlightenment) everything appears to be separate. There are subjects and objects. Such as mountains.

Then, suddenly, during meditation, a shift occurs, and the true empty nature of everything is revealed and you see that there really are no mountains, only an empty appearance of mountains. You now see through the illusory nature of things. It's pure consciousness *disguised* as mountains!

Then, after some time, after this truth sinks in, mountains are mountains once again, but now you know the truth, you know the secret meaning to life. You know the mountain is a mountain again, but that it's made of love. Of You. It's made of You.

No need to climb the mountain. *You are it!*

Silence and stillness are your Sherpas!

Tat tvam asi. Thou art that.

There are no longer problems or conflicts. There are only situations. All is silent and still, until that busy monkey mind kicks in again. What needs to be done is for you to melt yourself into stillness, pour yourself into beauty, dissolve yourself into wonder, and thus begin the secret hidden journey homeward to the true heart of existence.

YOUR TRUE POINT OF VIEW IS FROM ETERNITY

You're reading this book from the point of view of space and time, but the True You is eternity itself. In some way you have pierced time and space from eternity. You honestly know nothing of death, but you are now trapped seemingly helplessly in a body and world of decay and transience.

You are pure imagination that is unaware that you are pure imagination. You are pure imagination trapped in its own imaginings, seemingly powerlessly seduced by its own inventive construction.

Right now, if you haven't awakened, you cannot envision this to be so. It's unimaginable to you from your point of view in the phenomenal world, in your rotting, ephemeral body assembled and stitched together by time and space.

In order to awaken, you must become aware that what you truly are is pure awareness itself. You must become aware that you are awareness. You must become conscious of pure consciousness, conscious of your own consciousness.

Consciousness conscious of itself!

This is what this book will help you do.

Becoming Lucid

Lucid dreaming is the ability to wake up while you're dreaming, to actually wake up within the dream itself. If you start to meditate and play around with lucid dreaming techniques you will come to notice something quite bewildering.

When we dream at night we open up and create this amazing dream world of characters. For example, imagine that tonight you dream you are a doctor and you are treating people in a hospital.

It all seems so real, so vivid. But when you awaken from the dream, the whole thing vanishes, like a wisp of smoke! The hospital, the people, the needles, the stethoscope, the nurses, the beds and even you as the doctor, all disappear. Poof, awaken and it's all gone!

You realize upon awakening that all of it was simply made up of your consciousness, all of it, even the sky high hospital building, was merely made of dream stuff. But for a while there, it was the realest thing there ever was! Now you wake up into waking life, which is also like a dream, and there is your bed and there are your books and maybe your cat and your breakfast is there in the fridge waiting to be cooked, along with your coffee waiting to be brewed, and your friends are calling and you look outside and there are the birds and the bees and the flowers and the clouds and the trees and all of these things just seem *so real.*

To Truly Awaken from the Dream of Separation

But when there is an awakening from the dream of waking life, you truthfully realize that what you thought was you and me and your books and your cat and the clouds and the trees and the whole world are really appearances all made in and made of pure consciousness, pure awareness, pure imagination.

You *are* this imagination.

It's all you, it's all made up of the dreamer of the dream, all pure imagination endlessly being seduced by its own imaginings and to witness this, to experience this and to know this brings pure peace, total bliss, true oneness, utter wholeness.

It's the true meaning of *know thyself.*

The problem is that most of the time, almost all of the time, we are treading on the wheel of life like a hyper hamster, we're blindly running on the dream wheel, thinking we're awake and going about our business and then going to sleep at night and dreaming the dream within the dream, only to seemingly "awaken" in the morning into once again the waking dream and doing it all over again and then at night heading right back to the sleeping dream, and then come morning it's right back to the waking dream thus one never comes to the supreme comprehension that *both* are dreams.

Back to Basics

So just to review, the material level of anything is the lowest level of its appearance. This is just the surface, but certainly not the essence.

The first thing one must do is to detach from it. Detach from the seemingly physical. Then one must detach from the idea of a separate self, a self separate from all. Then ultimately even detach from detachment.

The essence of everything is pure consciousness.

One must come to see that time and space are only in the mind, but that unity and wholeness are your true nature. Time and space and this appearance of a physical world blanket your wholeness, cloud your unity, the unity in which the appearance makes its appearance in the first place. Astounding indeed.

There is no multiplicity, only an appearance of assortment.

The great psychologist and Zen master Dr. Stephen Wolinsky warns us that our brains only allow about .000054% of stuff to enter into our minds. Everything else is filtered out. He has us imagine seeing the world through a quantum lens where we'd see an occasional particle zipping by every now and then and one hell of a lot of empty space most of the time.

99.99999999999999999%

Now imagine that all of that small amount that seeps into our consciousness, the .000054% that we call reality, is really, at bottom, pure imagination. Well, when we do look deep down into the very heart of things, we find that it's all empty space. Any physicist will tell you that an atom is 99.9% empty! It's all space. Compressed space, emptiness compressed into mere vibration.

Again, think of a dream you may have tonight. In that dream, everything is constructed out of your consciousness.

Well, if you were a character "living" in that dream, then you would believe it all to be solid, including your very own body, brain, and self. But the truth is that all of it, your body, the cars, the houses, the flowers, the people - they're all made out of dream stuff, pure imagination.

So, there truly would not be a self in your "dream-you" and there wouldn't be any actual solidity to anything, we'd just know that it's all just a dream.

Your dream.

There would be no true essence, except that all of it is made of consciousness, and only one consciousness, the dreamer's. Yours. Yet, in the dream, the characters would all seem to have their own separate consciousnesses. They would each have a sense of self and they would experience fear and happiness and love and they would all be keenly aware of time and space, even though there clearly would not be any separate world of space or time in the dream.

Once You, the dreamer, awaken, poof, like magic, it all goes away. The whole dream, the whole world, and everyone and everything in it vanish into thin air. The whole thing was just made out of one substance and that one substance is consciousness.

Well, the whole universe sits in that.

You are that!

Congratulations.

YOUR TRUE NATURE

Upon awakening, a pure knowing enters. You understand at once that all of this life was a dream. You recognize at once that there is only knowing.

Knowing knowing itself.

You become it, the knowing. You *are* it. You know everything because you are everything, thus you know your True Self. Time and space cease to exist. Any dread of death passes away, because there really isn't any death, never mind birth!

It was all a powerfully convincing dream of separation. Separation from your True Nature.

True realization is the knowing that You are it, that the whole thing is You, and that this You is pure consciousness, pure imagination beyond the powerfully persistent deceptions of space-time.

This whole world is your dream. Whew!

You dreamt it up, you are the dreamer, but you've gone astray and are now convinced that you are separate. You're convinced that you are a separate person. Separation is the problem, separation is the nature of the dream. Your true nature is only wholeness. Oneness. Unity.

KNOWING KNOWING ITSELF

All great minds eventually come to this thought: Eternity is within you.

It is you. You are it. This and only this is permanent.

This is what you have been searching for in every cookie you eat, every store purchase, every desire or pleasure you have striven for, every relationship you've had, every trip you've ever booked. You are pure imagination, without cause, without a beginning or an end.

As Schopenhauer and the Buddha have urged, deny the urge, deny the Will, deny desire, for this world *is your idea,* your dream, your imagination. When we dream at night, we open up an entire universe in our minds, one that is made purely from our own consciousness. That's the hint. Take a hint. There's your clue!

We do it every night.

Wake up.

KILLING TIME

Forget time. There is only the ever-present now. Time and space dissolve into the now. The false self melts away in the power of the now. In total silence, in stillness, this can be achieved.

Don't miss this.

Everything you've ever seen, done, eaten, loved, was in the now. It's every moment. There's only now. Be absolutely mindful of this and the ego dream gently dissolves into the pure consciousness which is imagining it. Wholeness, boundless, spacious infinite awareness is your true nature.

Eternity isn't forever, it isn't time reaching out forever.

Eternity is the *stoppage of time*. Of illusions of past, of future.

The eternal now is all there really is.

This!

Dream Architecture

Just as in the sleeping dream we experience nightly, in the waking dream that we think of as real existence the seemingly separate individuals and objects are merely dream figures, lacking free will or volition of their own.

The dream character is exactly that, a fabrication of imagination and is not actually real at all, only temporarily or provisionally real within the dream.

At night, when you dream, I bet you think you're the dreamer of your dreams. This is just simply not the case. There isn't any real dreamer of your night dreams or the waking dream of existence.

There is only imagination. *You are that.*

These dreams are merely appearances within pure imagination, which is a no-thing. To call yourself a person is not personal identity, but rather *mistaken identity*. Your real identity, your True Self appears when a shift in point of view occurs after dropping the dream and waking up. Immediately, there is no doubt that it was all a dream and nothing really happened. Nothing has ever happened. It was all illusion, all pure imagination distorted and seduced by its own imaginings.

A Shift from Finity to Infinity!

When meditating, as the dissolution of your ego occurs, it will feel as if you are dying, because in a sense, you are. But don't forget it is only an illusion which is dying and once the illusory ego is out of the way your True Self appears, like a beautiful blue sky when dark clouds dissipate.

This is a profound shift and it is by far the greatest thing there is and ever was, great beyond words. It is a shift in identity from the point of view of the small finite self to the infinite True Self which you really are.

A shift from finity to infinity!

When this occurs, a *tremendous knowing* sets in that grows over time. This knowing is a shift from the finite to your infinite nature and it melts away all fear, all negativity, all worry, because all of that only comes with the false dream of separation as a separate self. That is where pain and suffering and anxiety and sadness come from, from thinking that you are not who you truly are, from being away from your true nature.

Sounds wild, doesn't it? But it is the only true thing you need to know.

Promise!

PEEKABOO!

There is only pure imagination. There is no *you*. There is only pure imagination dreaming *you* up, imagining you, and you are lost in the imagination of yourself! Who dreamt it up? You did! But not the ego *you*, not the little you with a name, but the true You.

See the difference?

One's illusory and finite and the other is infinite and is pure goodness itself. When you truly see this, when you directly experience this (which you will), then you will see that there really is no suffering out there, only an appearance or an illusion of suffering, because everyone out there is really You in disguise!

This is an astonishing realization.

When you are in a crowd, all of those eyes trained on you are your eyes because there is no "I". Just you, imagining the universe as your idea.

Again, it's a tremendously cosmic game of peekaboo! Peekaboo. I see you!

The veil of illusion is the costume covering up your True Self, making it seem that there is multiplicity and individuality. This separation is illusory and very painful.

WHAT A NEWSFLASH!

Your true identity is not your brain or your body or your name. Science, especially neuroscience, has been showing us that there is no self. Science has been showing us that matter is really empty. Couple this with meditation, which offers experiential evidence that this is true. When this false self or ego illusion truly vanishes, you see who you truly are.

Remember, these are merely, as Hamlet so eloquently put it, words, words, words...

Like eating the menu rather than the meal. Like sitting on the map rather than on the territory.

Direct experience is the only game in town. Know your True Self. To truly know yourself, one must meditate in stillness, in silent darkness. When this is done and all thoughts are gone, something beyond astonishing occurs. This and only this is the true purpose of yoga. Look it up! This is the only true purpose here in this place.

Wake up, dear reader.

Realize!

Know thyself!

DESIRE

Impermanence is the law of the land here, it's how this place functions. Everything you love will evaporate eventually. Nothing lasts. Yet, we are programmed or conditioned to continue to desire thing after thing, to seek experience after experience, to chase pleasure after pleasure. To pursue one more this, one more that. The reason for this is very clear once you awaken from the dream of separation.

Every pursuit of pleasure was merely you trying to become whole again, you trying to put an end to the separation, you just searching and trying to be, well, *You.* Making matters even worse, the "you" that you think you are isn't the true you, it is a fiction, a sham, a lie, an illusion, a mirage, a hallucination.

You are a fiction that doesn't know it's a fiction.

Once you are able to discern this and you are able to drop the "I" delusion, then the whole thing comes crumbling down and what is left is the most beautiful, most joyful knowledge that exists.

HAVE A BALL

Imagine if you went to a costume party, but at some point everyone drinks some stuff and they start to believe the costumes are for real, that they and the other guests are their masked representations and not their true selves underneath. The party might become a nightmare. No one would truly know one another and they wouldn't even know themselves. Maybe in the backs of their minds they would remember their true identities, but mainly these would be covered up in costume and anxiety.

Now imagine that you came to know the truth, that all is well, that really underneath all of the masks and the veils and the costumes are loving people and friends, but that they are just lost. Well, here is your chance to see the truth behind this enormous costume ball we call Existence. The truth will set you free, they say.

Damn right it will. It isn't an easy task. The world around us seems so real, but I'm arguing that this assumption that we make at a very young age that reality is solid, that matter and the physical world is the only true reality, is dead wrong and quite deadly.

It is death its very self.

Materialism is death.

We think that matter and the world are real.

We are wrong. But it takes some unraveling to see this. The idea of no-self is evidently no self-evident idea!

Far from it. But, all of the evidence points to it.

Endless Perfection

So, you want my advice, dear reader? Now that you know them, try to forget all the terms and definitions laid out in this book. The real truth is, *there's nothing real here. It's all pure imagination.* As Shakespeare said, it's all the same stuff that dreams are made of. If and when you try this and the dream dissolves, what's left is the endless consciousness, what's left is infinite intelligent space. The ego can only understand complexity.

But, the truth is there is nothing complex in actual reality. This strange dream is just like a very compelling mirage or hologram. It is all a simple dream of separation that evolved in the middle of non-conceptual endlessness.

Liken it to a complex drawing in the sand at the beach. Endless complexity is possible, sure. But the solution here is simple, yet not easy to do. The solution to this mystery is to just realize it's *all* sand.

It's all pure imagination. Pure consciousness.

The Nature of the Dream

The natural evolution of the dream is to wake up to its true nature, which is endless, spacious, ecstatic consciousness, pure consciousness without a head or a body or a world.

Any and all other questions about the how's and why's of all this is merely the ego trying to preserve itself through the endless pondering of ideas and concepts. It is your every thought that blocks the light, just as the ripples on a pond hide its stillness or as clouds hide the view of an endless blue sky.

Your mission: Drop it all.

How endless pure imagination created the imagined illusion of solid stuff out of infinite emptiness is the galactic granddad of all magic tricks.

The Ultimate Paradigm Shift

Don't get me wrong, I know how difficult this idea is to swallow. This is the biggest paradigm shift one can ask a human to accept, bigger than slavery, gay rights, and women's rights, bigger than anything anyone has ever had to imagine.

What I can say is that the certitude of the materialist position will be replaced by an even greater certitude of nonduality and once you wake up from the dream of separation and when both paradigms can be "seen" side by side it becomes patently obvious which state is primary and which state is the dream. In the moment of silence and stillness when all thought is stopped, there is no "you", there is only the infinite. "You" are out and your true presence is felt, which is only loving joy. This is most certainly what people call "god", but it isn't some bearded being in the sky.

It is the true You and this shadow world is merely your dream and all is well because none of it ever really happened. From this point of view, from the point of view of eternity, *there is only You*, the one mind knowing itself, which is only pure infinite love.

You are eternal, there's no bottom to You.

The Same View As the Sages

Yet, right now, you think this is real. You'd bet your life on it. But the fact is that you are god and this is your dream. You're doing it all. You're everyone, pretending not to know you're everyone.

When the "I" drops, you are right there, waiting, you never really left. The "I" must shatter and then, there you are. There is not a person, there is only an open window. An opening, a tear in the veil. You only greet yourself. In astonishment. This is not religion, not even a philosophy. It is what Buddha taught. What Lao Tzu taught. What Jack Kerouac wrote novels and novels about. It is every lecture by the great Alan Watts. Every poem by every Sufi, such as Rumi or Hafiz or Kabir.

It's the very same idea. Religions point to it and it is the truth they all try to attain. This is the oneness you've heard people speak about. The wholeness. It's the realization that there is only oneness. This is nonduality. There is no self. No separation. No "I". The ego is the veil between the illusory "you" and the true You which is boundless.

THE SUBJECT-OBJECT FAÇADE

The idea of a separate subject and an object is a facade. The whole point is to wake up and see this. This oneness. What you realize is unity. You realize that you *are* this, and that this is love, you realize that love is your true nature. To wake up and to know that your pursuit of love and happiness here is really a longing for returning home to the heart, to nirvana, to the endless everything that you already are, but don't know that you are, because you're caught in this strange dream of thought and separation.

The only way to attain this is through meditation in complete silence, with all thought totally ceasing. It's astonishing when you wake up to your true nature. This is what people call Heaven. This is what Buddhists call Nirvana.

Nirvana means extinction and this is dying to what you think you are and realizing what you truly are, realizing your true nature, beyond words. And to try and share this with you? It's effing the ineffable!

Could it be that I am wrong and that I am just imagining this? No. Absolutely not.

But every single other thing is imagination.

Every single other thing is folly.

Now, how the heck do I get Randi to understand awareness isn't in the brain? *That the brain is in awareness!* Whoa!

SUFFERING AS A TEACHER

We go through our lives and we think we must not suffer and we try to avoid suffering at all costs. We desire things and move towards pleasure and we run from suffering at all costs, meanwhile we are suffering, the suffering is already here, it's the dream, it's the nature of the dream, which is finite, hence the suffering. To wake up from this dream is to put an end to pain, an end to all suffering. Once you know this, once you *are* this, you can only suffer if you forget yourself. If you forget who you truly are. Suffering is seeking wholeness or completeness, it is not realizing you are wholeness and completeness its very self.

Knowing your true nature puts you in the position of being in a good mood for eternity. Pain teaches finiteness, it is limited. Pain is good because it exposes the *one* that can be *in* pain. When there is no self, there is *no one* there to suffer. Desire isn't as bad as the desirer.

Just think, many people's days or weekends are ruined by a little rain. When you wake up, for real, you will see that rain is just you giving yourself bath. A bath of love! You will be all heart. The heart always chooses love. It is love. The mind chooses fear, the fear of the end of separation.

DON'T FORGET!

It is as if the whole world has Alzheimer's disease. The whole world has forgotten who it is, forgotten its True Self. The One Self. The world *is* love. It was born *from* love. It is a manifestation *of* love. It must return *to* love. The True Self gave birth to the world. But we have forgotten. We have forgotten that we are love and we've forgotten how to get back home.

The world is the movie in the space of the True Self, it's the shadow, it's its manifestation. It's the play. It's the show. But the mind comes up and forgetting sets in. You get lost in the role of a separate self. You forget your true nature. You think that you are real and that you are on your own.

So you spend your entire life searching for love and peace and wholeness. This is really you searching for yourself. Searching for what you have forgotten. Love is knowing your True Self. Love is nonduality. Love is oneness. Never two! Never multiplicity. Love is wholeness. Love is unity, it is the forgetting of the separation illusion. Temporarily or eternally.

For many years I explored and loved Buddhism, Zen, and Taoism, but I never really got their true meaning, which is that when the mind is totally silent and there is no thinking whatsoever, then the illusion of a separate self drops and "you" realize your true nature beyond space and time and you see that your true nature is not the body but pure consciousness, pure imagination.

This state is called Buddha Mind. One Mind. The philosopher Immanuel Kant called it the noumenal world. All else is mere appearance. Shadows on Plato's cave wall. Kant called that shadow world the phenomenal world. The phenomenal world and the noumenal world are two sides of the same coin.

This is exactly what the Sufi poets like Rumi and Hafiz wrote thousands of poems about. This is something very hard to put in words, one must have direct experience of this, and it is the only way to achieve enlightenment. Once direct experience occurs, all is well always. This is called realization, satori, or enlightenment. It is the awakening from the dream of separation.

I used to like to say that we humans put a lot of stuff in front of us to block out death, to block out the gravestone that awaits us. Things, money, art, literature, hobbies, relationships, etc. Distractions to make us not think of what was waiting at the end of the road. Little did I know then that all of the stuff we use to clog or distract or shield us from our mortality, actually does the opposite!

It clogs up your knowing that you are immortal. It clogs up your knowing that your true nature is eternal. What a journey we all take. The truth is we were here before the Sun was set a light! Before the stars were blazing! Whew.

I'm over here now! Fear is not knowing yourself. Not knowing your true nature is love. Getting caught up thinking this is all real.

Love is all, which alone is Truth. Love is Truth. Truth truly is Beauty.

If you truly could see once and for all how beautiful you are, if you caught just a *glimpse* of the real You, you would burst into tears of joy! Then later, when you recognized your True Self in others, you would see that it's like witnessing the most beautiful flowers in the world *just exploding open, just bursting forth, blossoming for you all day long.*

Talk about The Garden of Eden! Paradise, right here, right now.

But words don't cut it. It must be experienced. As the great Thomas Merton wrote, there's just no clear way of telling people that they're all walking around *shining like the sun!*

Love - just be that, dear friend.

All day and night people should send love to each other. Everyone wants it because every one is *the one* underneath the coverings of ego.

Night and day. Night after night. Hearts to each other. Reminders of who they truly are.

THE ILLUSION OF FREEWILL

Do we have freewill? The true meaning of free will isn't that you could have done otherwise. The real meaning of freedom of the will is *to be free of willing altogether.* This and only this leads to liberation. To achieve this, we must overthrow the granddaddy of all dualisms, that between created and creator.

No faith is required here. Direct experiential evidence is readily available to anyone who seeks it. Maybe mystics have direct experience because they can't have faith. People have faith because they don't know about this or can't attain direct experience.

But the mystic knows. And now you know. This is why happiness doesn't last, why it is so ephemeral. Because true joy doesn't rely on circumstances. Only knowing who you are will do it. Empty your "self" out, carve yourself into an empty vessel, let the truth in and let the words out.

Gently dissolve into mist, be light-headed.

THINKING ABOUT THINKING

You think this world is real because you're always at it. Always thinking of it. Always thinking. You're thinking right now. Stop thinking. *Just stop.* Stop thinking of it all and it will vanish like a wisp of smoke into thin air. You won't just know joy, you won't merely know love, you will *be* joy, and you will *be* love.

Find your true self and you are joy knowing the knower! What have you got to lose? You've got everything to lose! And nothing to gain! Imagine what it will feel like to realize all this time you thought you were the shadow, that you were really the sun!

Think of any problem you have right now. Any worry. Whatever it is, it's your false self. The true you is free. It is joyous. Seek that. Know thy true self. Discover you. Dive deep within. Become free. None of this you see around you is real. It's all pure imagination.

Everything you think, everything you believe, is really a projection of your own imagination. Cease all contact with thoughts, objects and ideas.

As Shakespeare had Hamlet say, there is no good or bad, *it's thinking that makes it so.*

Surrender totally. Be pure. Be unattached. Find the source of these thoughts and concepts. Seek the source of mind. There You are! Strip naked and see what happens. Slowly remove the layers and layers of thought that cover You. Strip down naked before The Void.

Take it all off. Remove it. Empty the mind. Stand completely naked and just watch what happens. Once it all stops, there is no need for words. There's no person, no ego, no self. No past, no future. No time, no space. You, who you truly are, are no longer bound by endless chains of words and concepts. Nothing can hold you. You are free. Boundless.

Sounds wild.

Until it happens to you.

Dream Dialogue Seven

❦

Me: Wow, look at that moon! (points)

Randi: (looks at his apprentice's finger, jokingly, then follows his gaze up slowly to the full moon hanging like ripened fruit in the sky)

Me: Ha! Yes, don't you get caught looking at that finger and forget to see that gorgeous moon!

Randi: Let's not forget Galileo, either. What a courageous man he was!

Me: Whew! I was just about to bring him into our conversation! How in the world did you know!?

Randi: (smiles) They don't call me The Amazing Randi for nothing, Jimmy.

Me: You truly are amazing. As was, Galileo. Here was a man of courage, he wasn't afraid. He made this piece of glass, like a prosthetic eye, that changed the world, shifted everything! Shook the very foundations of this great globe!

Randi: Yes, yes, wonderful, wonderful!

Me: You know how you offer that One Million Dollar Prize? Well, I'm prepared to offer you a challenge. A challenge to be as courageous as our man Galileo. And a chance for you to look through a telescope of your very own!

I promise what you will see, what you will experience directly, is that this world is an illusion. A dream.

Randi: (looks at the door)

Me: Oh no, you stay put, Mr. Amazing. Take a look through the telescope...

Randi: I don't see a telescope.

Me: (holds out both closed fists) Pick a hand, any hand...

Randi: (chuckles) This one, the left!

Me: (slowly opens the left hand, revealing a mala, Buddhist meditation beads)

Meditation is a telescope, one of several, which you can use as tool to see through to the Truth. To see the moon.

Randi: Subjective...

Me: Direct! Direct experience. Come on, be a true skeptic, go all the way into this thing.

Randi: (shakes a finger at me)

Me: I'm your student. You taught me how to be a true skeptic. You taught me very well.

Randi: What's in the other hand?

Me: (slowly opening my hand to reveal a small colorful pill)

Take this and you will see how deep and amazing the rabbit hole truly is...

Randi: Pills? Drugs? Illegal!

Me: This right here is what you call a true paradigm popper. Just like Galileo and his glass, which was also illegal, for which he was arrested for and why he spent the rest of his life toiling away in the Vatican basement, of all places!

Randi: This is different.

Me: Oh really now? To me, they are the same!

Don't you want to find out how something came from nothing?

Don't you want to see how you get something seemingly solid from absolutely nothing?

Be an honest skeptic, Randi. Explore and challenge ALL important assumptions.

Galileo did. He risked his life. Giordano Bruno lost his life, he was barbecued alive! The mystic Marguerite Porete was so sure that consciousness is prior to matter that when the Church decided to burn her alive at the stake she walked to her own death with a joyous smile on her face and her confidence scared the ignorant men who were to light her on fire.

Well, I, too, risked my life for skepticism. For Truth.

For a glimpse at that moon. That illuminating Truth.

Randi: I'll never take that.

Me: Ah, but you see, you already have. What did you think was in that glass of water I handed you earlier?

Randi: Noooooooooo!

Randi wakes up in his bed, in a sweat. Alas, it was only another dream.

Randi: Drat! Double drat!!

◈

CHAPTER 7

Sacred Outlaws

THE WORD CIRCUS

So, ARE YOU JUST ABOUT ready to put all the books down, call off the search, and take this journey deep within yourself? Are you prepared to leave the shallow waters of the mind? Are you prepared to pay attention to your breath and to dive deep down underneath the veil to the true heart of being?

As mystic Thomas Merton asked, what's the point of sailing to the moon if we aren't able to cross the abyss that separates us from our true selves?

Trust me, it isn't as easy as it sounds. For years and years now you have invented an entire universe made out of words. This universe is merely your idea. Want to know this for certain? Well, stop the word circus in your head and see what happens. Just once. Just once look deeply at the apparatus you have created to make this show of words, concepts, and ideas. Just this once, look.

I don't care how you do it, just drop your mind. Still it. Calm it. Too much thinking is the problem. You must make your mind *quiescent*. This is the secret of life. Do whatever it takes, whatever method works best. Do not attach to your thoughts. The whole point here is to still the mind. When the mind is finally laid to rest, realization will happen. When thoughts are silenced, you will return home.

MEDITATION AND MEDICINE

So here's the deal. To get to this most beautiful realization, it takes meditation and if you're lucky it can happen pretty quickly. Or it can take years. The first time I broke through, it was pure silent meditation.

But the next time I had a total breakthrough I used a tool to help me get there, a tool called mdma. Most kids use this at raves and yes raves can be a kind of a collective meditation, but to do mdma in silent darkness is to twiddle some serious knobs and dials on your consciousness and to cleanse the doors of perception in a very powerful way.

It softens and then dissolves the illusion of the self and doing so dissolves what you thought were your boundaries, allowing you to merge with the great mystery that you truly are. This breakthrough is the most beautiful thing there is and don't forget that every one of your searches for pleasure is really a search for this, for You.

Now, some people, especially academics, may object to a meditation tool such as a puff of marijuana or a pill of mdma. Yet, many of these same people smoke, due to stress, or drink coffee, or drink alcohol and take pills for aches and pains and depression. These are all temporary alleviations, whereas awakening from the dream of separation is a permanent cure.

A permanent cure. That is worth taking some yogi medicine, isn't it?

Are you going to miss out on the most important thing there is for you to investigate in your short time here? Look at Raymond Smullyan, amazing mind, logician, read all the books on this thing, even wrote books on it, yet he writes that he still doesn't know *for sure* if it's true. But his philosophy has made him a wonderfully loving and warm human being, so kind, so generous, so free from drama and nonsense, really living in the present as much as possible.

And yet, perhaps he missed it. Don't miss it, my dear reader. Don't miss you!

Take Doug Hofstadter. He's right there, right on it, yet he thinks he's finite. Finite! And chooses to remain finite, even if he was faced with evidence to the contrary, because he would then lose himself. But, that's the whole point! Lose the self, the fiction that he said was a hallucination, an illusion, yet he clings to it even in the face of the truth.

Don't give in to fear. It's an illusion. What did Bob Dylan say? The sun isn't yellow...it's chicken! Move towards love.

In the 1960's they conducted research into all of this. They recently repeated the original study, this time at Johns Hopkins University. Researchers used psilocybin in a proper and peaceful setting, giving it to patients who all had an intense fear of death. After a few hours the patients reported that it felt like their chests were opening and that their hearts were filling up with pure love and that they had a true feeling of oneness with everyone and the whole cosmos. Most said they no longer feared death. Asked afterwards, months and years later, most reported that the experience had transformed their lives for good and that their fear of death was gone and they now felt very connected to the universe.

These were ordinary people that had never taken a psychedelic in their lives. Totally transformed. Cocooned caterpillars into boundless butterflies.

Prisoners in jail who were recently released were given this holy medicine. These were real convicts, ones that usually would wind up right back in jail. After taking the psychedelic medicine, most, if not all, never went back to jail. It changed their lives in a loving and moral way and they became good citizens due to this powerful experience. Why?

Well how can you cheat or hurt others when you now know they are truly You? So, knowing this, and guided by silent meditation, or with the help of some tools, let's proceed full steam ahead onwards and upwards into eternal love!

This is no easy task. Simple seeming. But the hardest simple there is! The tenacious motherfucker (The TMF!) of an ego does not want to die. It will be tough to get rid of it. Is there anything really there to get rid of? Watch this in silence and find out. Your true nature is the space between thoughts. You reside in the space between words. You are space. That's your true nature. The space in which all of this takes place. When you drop all thoughts, in total silence, show me your mind.

Do not try to attain. Your true nature is always present. Joy is always present. Just remove the blockage, remove the veil. Let go. Surrender. This happens in total silence. Keep quiet and watch how the chatter of the monkey mind slows to a halt. Then watch what happens. Just stop. Be still. Don't move. *Stop.* Don't think. Stay in silence. Go deeper. Drop the world for one minute. Watch what happens. Stop thought. This is true meditation. It's not for alleviating stress. Forget hot yoga! Find your true nature. This is meditation. Being still. This is true freedom.

Give up the quest. Watch what happens. Stop. Greet the present moment.

You've never been truly present.

Do it now. Desire will drop. What is left? Don't stir. Silent. Still. Drop everything. *Even these words.* Let go. Fall into silence. Fall from the mind to the heart. You are bottomless, fathomless, boundless, and spacious. You can't grasp it, *you are it.* You are awareness aware of itself.

See what does the *seeing* and *know* what does the *knowing.* Don't observe, *be* what does the *observing.*

Be the witness, not the thoughts.

UNRAVEL

My friend Dori-Jo, a talented musician and wonderful person, had the following questions when we first discussed the mysterious tremendum together.

Question: If waking up from a dream brings us back to what we see now, then what's there when we wake up from this?

Every morning we awaken from our night dreaming into a waking dream, a waking life. Upon true awakening, you realize you are awareness itself.

You see that you were pure imagination/pure consciousness, lost in its own imaginings.

There's only endless blissful awareness.

This is very hard to explain in words. Words fail. Concepts fail. But they point to the Truth. Ever hear that Chinese expression it's like a finger pointing at the moon?

Try to imagine a shift in consciousness where you realize that you don't exist in a body. That your body exists in you! It's a profound shift! It's true astonishment. Imagine knowing that you don't exist in the world. *That the real picture here is that the world exists in you!*

The finger pointing at the moon is this: If I pointed at the moon and you stared at my finger and not the moon, you'd miss the amazing moon. So say the moon represents Truth. The finger represents words and concepts. So only the foolish get caught up in the words, rather than following them to the Truth. Don't miss what the words are pointing to.

> *Question: But, if we are only here as something that is being "dreamt" by a sort of supreme consciousness, then what is the point of it all? If dreams tell us something about our own psyche and subconscious, then what does this "dream" say about the entity that dreams it? Why is this happening at all?*

It's happening because *you* are dreaming it. You *are* that supreme consciousness. You're just veiled right now. The way to know if it's a dream is to wake up. Forget the how. Just that it's here is the mystery of mysteries. The mystery is everywhere. Look around.

I'm here to remind you that all is okay, always. That all is well, and then some! And that you're IT.

> *Question: But does the fact that "I" or "we" am/are dreaming it (wow) mean anything? Is it just a meaningless dream or could it be a way of this supreme consciousness that we all are a part of trying to better itself in a way? A while ago when I was into this I got to thinking that we all*

are a little piece of that supreme consciousness and we're sent here as human beings to learn compassion and goodness and once you've really understood it then that piece of the whole goes back to the whole, did that make any sense?

That makes perfect and beautiful sense. You're certainly onto it. But again, these are mere words. Like the finger, they point to the truth, but they are not the truth.

What you are is only perfection. Wholeness. Compassion. Love. Try to imagine it all as you, from the point of view of eternity, lost as you say, in little pieces, like characters in a grand cosmic play (wonder why we love theater so much!) and all of those pieces are what we think of as others, as separate, but they are you, the theater set is you, the whole shebang. All you.

The way to know this is to wake up. The way to wake up is to drop the "I"/ego/veil and *see your true face.* You have to empty the "self" out. In stillness. In silence. No thought. No chatter.

Then you will realize it's all a play and that you're playing every part!

But again, these are merely words, words, words. With words, it is like you are eating the menu picture and not eating the meal. Visiting the map, but not the territory.

And anything good here, anything loving, compassionate, beautiful, sublime, *is* the pure imagination, the supreme consciousness, *you,* appearing metaphorically, through art, music, a kind gesture, a look, a feeling - it's all you, shining through. This is why it feels so good, this is why love is all you need, this is why.

Because deep down, our true nature is love and that very love is oneness, wholeness, and any suffering here is the illusion that we are, as you pointed out, in pieces. That's the dream, one of separation, and everything we do here is a striving to be whole again.

But, the truth is, you're really always whole, you can't not be. It's just that the false self, the veil, the tenacious mother of an ego, makes it seem that way, like a hallucination.

Suffering is separation from your True Self. Again. Words, words, words. Until you experience it, have direct experience.

Question: But what's the point of creating something that puts the self through such pain? If we are all the supreme consciousness and the supreme consciousness created the world that we're living in then why is there so much pain and suffering inflicted on the being that created it?

All of the pain in the world comes from not knowing who and what you truly are. Once you know this, once you shift identity from the ego self to your True Self and true knowing, pure knowing, *knows itself,* the game changes.

In knowing thyself, you become aware of your True Self, which is indestructible and untouchable by suffering. This is the true end of suffering.

It's as if the suffering never happened. You clearly see that what you thought was suffering was merely a shadow of the one true thing.

The true you is never even aware of suffering. It can't be. It's only pure infinite perfection. Oneness *is* love. Multiplicity *is* suffering. Sounds wild! Until you see it. The duality between the creator and creature has to be dropped. Oneness is achieved. This is love. The suffering occurs because you forgot just who you truly are and you were caught up in the dream of separation. You just want to get home.

Question: But why did we create all this in the first place?

Always go back to how a dream works. Think of a dream you may have tonight. Imagine you dream you and I are on a mountain top, discussing this very same thing. Those dream bodies of yours and of mine are made of pure imagination, your imagination, your consciousness. So is the mountain, the moon, the stars in the dream, all created from dream stuff, consciousness, it's all pure imagination.

Then you wake up and in an instant I'm gone. The mountain is gone. You've moved a mountain! Where did I go and where did you put that tremendous mountain?

The answer is - we never were. It never happened, there was an appearance, only provisionally. It was all just a dream.

So back to your question, there is no reason why. You fell asleep. You forgot who you were for a bit and during that time you became mountains and the moon and me and you, and we were discussing the mystery of it all. So it goes.

Question: If nothing is real then why does pain feel more real than anything else?

Suffering is being caught up in the dream of separation. You suffer when that happens because you are identifying with the little but tenacious ego rather than with your True Self.

See it like a costume party where you play every role. If you really get lost in the role, and forget your True Self, your true nature, and get caught up in that tenacious ego, then you're lost and far from home. Waking up, awakening, is coming home to your True Self, your true nature, and knowing beyond a doubt that you're IT, that you're the whole thing.

Once again, go back to how a dream works.

If you and I are in your dream tonight and we are suffering from all sorts of life problems and we don't know that it's only a dream, your dream, then we're going to be anxious and suffer and we might be sad and even in despair.

But, if we know it's a dream, well... then we *lighten up*! We will feel *illuminated* and we don't take it all so damn seriously. We will be determined to have fun and to even play in the dream and if and when we see others suffering around us, we will know all of those people are really made of *your* dream, *your* consciousness, *your* imagination, so we will try and cheer them up and somehow let them know it's all okay, because deep down, they are you.

For a lot of people, suffering becomes their teacher. It's what makes them finally drop the dream. And wake up. They finally give up, renounce it all, stop believing, desiring, and seeking in it, and get a taste of the noumenal, your true nature, which is beyond words and must be experienced directly.

Rather than avoid the suffering, go into the suffering. Go into the hole in your heart, the void, because that is *a tear in the fabric of the dream.* That's where *love* is, which is what "you" are. The suffering is ego-you not being able to find *You.* Lost. Separated. Caught in samsara, caught in the web. Many times when we suffer, we have a drink or watch something on television, or drown it out somehow. Dive in! Unravel!

⸎

Inner Wakefulness
By Rumi

This place is a dream
only a sleeper considers it real
then death comes like dawn
and you wake up laughing
at what you thought was your grief.
A man goes to sleep in the town
where he has always lived
and he dreams
he's living in another town
in the dream he doesn't remember
the town he's sleeping in his bed in
he believes the reality
of the dream town
the world is that kind of sleep.

Humankind is being led
along an evolving course,
through this migration
of intelligences
and though we seem
to be sleeping
there is an inner wakefulness,
that directs the dream
and that will eventually
startle us back
to the truth
of who we are.

This stateless state of inner wakefulness Rumi writes of is beyond the senses and beyond reason. It is the true oneness, an absolute knowing that there is no multiplicity, no form, and no separate self, for this is the True Self and you, dear reader, are that.

Dream Dialogue
Eight

❦

Randi and I are standing on an immense cliff and we are edging out towards the ledge.

Randi: Now, I know *this* is not a map, Jimmy.

Me: This is most certainly the territory. We're almost there!

Randi: Where are we going exactly?

Me: Where very few dare to go.

Randi: Okay, lead the way.

Soon everything they see seems to gently dissolve. Form is shown to be what it truly is, endless wondrous emptiness.

Me: We're now at the crumbling edge of reality.

Randi: Astonishing!

Me: Come on Randi, take it little further.

Randi: But there's no bottom to it...

Me: That's right. There's no bottom to *you*! Okay, we're at the very top of the mountain. Now keep climbing. One more step.

Randi: Unfathomable...

Me: Take the stepless step.

Randi: (reaches out, his hands stretching into endless emptiness)

Randi: Nothingness...

Me: (handing Randi a copy of The Skeptic's Apprentice) Come on, Randi! Try to hang a peg in the sky!

CHAPTER 8
Birth of a Bodhisattva

NO ONE GETS OUT ALIVE

IF YOU READ ONLY ONE book in your entire life, this is the book. This is it, your way out of the dream of separation. It's your ticket off the quivering meat wheel of suffering.

These words are working away like little hammers, hammering away at the blocks that you've built up to hide your true nature. Chipping away, block by block.

This book is really the one endless mind trying to convince its sleeping and dreaming self to wake up from its dream of finitude.

This experience is the most important discovery you can ever make. Let me tell you what it has taught me. Remember, again, words fail. But let's give it a try, shall we?

I used to have a serious fear of death. It was intense. Like the great philosopher Miguel Unamuno, I had a very tragic sense of life. I wanted so badly for this to all go on, for this consciousness to forever continue. I didn't want it to ever end. I read everything I could get my hands on. But it seemed as though there was no way out of death. As Jim Morrison would often say, no one gets out of here alive.

My library in my home has more books on death and dying than most folks' full libraries. I probably have more books on finitude or mortality than most public libraries carry on the subject. So yes, you can say I'm an expert on how we die. Some title, huh?

Now, all of that has drastically changed.

Now I *know* that what I truly am is indestructible. I know that this consciousness *does not* have an end. Ever. I know that I am eternal.

I know that all is well, *and then some!*

BOTTLED UP

I'm absolutely convinced now. I know it deep down in my zen bones.

This has made every day a wondrous event rather than a series of goodbyes. What I am is indestructible and the same goes for you. The only way to know this is to have the experience.

It's changed everything for only the good, *because the good is all that truly exists.*

Waking up is a profound and radical shift that takes the fictitious made up "you" out of the picture and suddenly the True You appears and you realize that not only are you one with everything, you *are* everything and everything is actually *made up of you.*

Imagine an empty bottle on a table. Imagine that you are convinced that what you are is the air in the bottle, confined by the boundaries of the glass. Then along comes a hammer (direct experience) and it smashes the bottle to pieces and the air in the bottle, *what you thought was you,* merges with the air outside of the bottle.

Suddenly you realize in an astonishing jolting flash that you are space, all space, not just the space seemingly imprisoned in the bottle!

You broke the spell.

Philosopher Daniel Dennett wrote a book on religion called *Breaking The Spell.* Well, direct experience is the true breaking of the spell, the spell that you are finite and separate. The spell is the veil, it is the pull of the world. The TMF, that tenacious mother of an ego. Break it like a bottle, shatter it, and voila! You're nothing and everything. You're pure imagination beyond space and place.

You are boundless, endless space, within and without, always and forever. You are it. The *whole* thing! The whole works! Holy! You are all that! The whole kit and caboodle! The whole ball of wax! The whole nine yards! The full Monty! Hook, line, and sinker! Lock, stock, and barrel! Wall to wall! Across the board! It's *all* You!

THE SEPARATION ILLUSION

Love is nonduality. Love is oneness. Never two. Never three. Never plurality, never multiplicity. There is only an appearance of that.

Love is wholeness. Period.

Love is seeing through the separation illusion. Temporarily or eternally. Love is knowing your true self.

Be the path, don't follow the path.

Forget the "Plath"!

Now where is Randi?

Time to slay the dragon of materialism once and for all. Time to tell Randi we were all wrong. Time to deliver the knockout punch of nonduality.

Down goes Randi, down goes Randi. But it's okay, because there is *no ground!* And there is *no Randi...!*

There is only the groundless ground of pure consciousness!

Ah, never mind Randi. If the Buddha himself showed up at my door and said James, I made a mistake, we were wrong about it all, I'd level him with a nice Zen smack to the cheek and tell him to go to the yard and get his ass back under a tree and to meditate until he got it right once and for all.

That convinced. More than convinced. More than knowing. I Am That! I am very aware, very aware that what I am and what we all are is pure awareness itself. Randi sure was right when he told me early on that *it's all about love!*

GOOD FORTUNE

Today I opened my chinese fortune cookie at dinner and it read:

"Teach only love because that is what you are."

Coincidence? I don't think so. Not anymore!

I sent a picture of it to Paul and he replied:

You should keep that! A note to your self from your infinite self. When's the last time you saw a cookie fortune like that?!

I wrote him back, telling him that it was *finity pointing at infinity!*

BRING ON JAMES RANDI

It is ON in the Void! Full steam ahead, onwards and upwards into eternal love! So what if Randi slams a door in my face? So what if he gives me a loving shot to the head with his cane? I now know why one can't be upset with others. I see it so clearly. It is because they are all you. The reality of the situation is that it is really *you* "upsetting" yourself. Astonishing!

There is only you. You greeting you, in disguise. Howdy!

Again, these are only words until you experience this transdimensional shift in identity and see it for yourself. Even then, it takes almost constant monitoring and revising of your awareness to be the open window, to realize and stay aware that it's all truly inside out. It is exciting to watch all this unfold! What a journey we're sharing. The awakening within grows more and more every day. Less and less "me" and more everything. Less "I" and more awareness. Always, always in astonishment!

Just think, endless pure imagination has created the imagined illusion of solid stuff, all out of out of infinite emptiness!

Forget magic! This is the mother of all magic tricks.

BIRTH OF A BODHISATTVA

Now that I know for certain that I am indestructible, that there is no bottom to me, that all is endless peace, I know that I want to help others know this freedom. This is a bodhisattva, a real life angel that can go into total enlightenment, but rather stays to alleviate the suffering of others.

I know and sense this compassion from deep within. Just as silence is calling me, it is calling. It's the same. I am more keenly aware than ever now that I must face my former teacher. Tell him that we were mistaken.

And then remind him and others who they truly are.

WORDS, WORDS, WORDS

Somehow I will find the words to tell Randi what has happened to his favorite apprentice. What he missed. The lesson he forgot long ago.

It's all a game of forget me not!

I will try and tell him that in the moment of silence and stillness when all thought is stopped, there is no "you", there is only the infinite and that the infinite is the True You. That what you thought of as "you" is out and your true presence is felt and undeniable.

This presence is only loving and joyous. This is what people call god, but it isn't some being in the sky, it's the True You and it's what *contains* the sky.

This shadow world is merely your dream and all is well because it never happened! From this point of view of eternity, there is only You, the one mind knowing itself, which is only pure infinite love.

You're eternal, dammit. *There is no bottom to you.* That's it!

You think this world is real. But really *you are god*. It has all been your dream. You're doing it. Don't forget. You're everyone. You're just pretending not to know.

When the "I" drops your true nature is right there waiting. You never left.

The "I" must shatter and then suddenly there You are, with no idea of anything separate! Pure oneness. Wholeness.

O Holy Night! The stars are brightly shining. A thrill of hope the weary world rejoices...

THE GOSPEL OF PURE ASTONISHMENT

Unity, perfect peace, and love is all there is. Shockingly, there is not a single person here, only an open window, a clearing, a fissure, a tear in the veil of ignorance and obliviousness.

Wherever you go, you only greet yourself. Once you truly know this, it's electrifying to watch it all unfold!

The gospel of astonishment states that no faith, belief, or religion is necessary. There is no church or mosque or temple.

Within your very temple is the temple! *You are the holy place.*

Religions point to it, this is the truth they all try to attain.

This is the oneness. The realization that there is only oneness. Advaita. Nonduality. Non atman, no-self. No "I". No separation at all. The ego is the veil between the illusory and the True You which is boundless. The idea of a subject and object is a facade. There's only pure imagination. You at that.

This is the gospel of astonishment!

BE LOVE

The whole point here is to wake up and see that you *are* love. Love is your true nature and your pursuit of happiness here is really a longing for returning home to the heart, to Nirvana, to the endless everything that you already are but just don't know it because you're caught up in the strange dream of thought and separation.

The only way to attain this is through meditation in complete silence with all thought totally stopped. It's astonishing when you wake up to your true nature. It's Heaven. It's Nirvana.

It's the true happy ending!

Nirvana really means extinction. It's the dying to what you think you are. *A person. A separate self.* It is the snuffing out of the illusory self and the astonishing realization of your true nature, beyond words.

It's f-ing ineffable!

All is holy. All is You. You are everything. When you awaken you wake up *to* infinity, *as* infinity. *Everything is holy.* Everything is the body of the Buddha. A penny. A blade of grass. The ocean. People. Animals. Insects. Cats. Gnats. Everything!

Even this book in your hands. It is the body of the Buddha.

Now you know that true joy doesn't rely on circumstances.

True joy is found only in the knowing of who you really are. Suffering is found only in the forgetting of who you really are. Let go of the mind and let go of all seeming troubles. What's left? The True You. The world is only your idea. The world is only in your mind. All seemingly bad things are only in your mind. Let go of the mind. There You are, you're always here.

You're always it. But you forget. There's nothing to become. You're already it. The whole shebang. You need to stay You, but learn to not be what you are not. Stop that. Everyone's it. Everyone makes up the pure consciousness.

The consciousness so pure *it doesn't need a brain.* The brain needs consciousness. Consciousness doesn't need anything.

Out of pure nothingness comes the imagination of ourselves as separate. Your job, your *only* job, is to awaken. Come together.

BECOMING THE TEACHER

Think about this: Imagine me telling you not to be upset with another person who has been bothering you and then imagine me wondering how much, at the time, you might know that the other person is really you.

While doing this I would have forgotten that you are also me. Whew. I'm in reality telling myself not to worry about the other person. Your worry is my worry. Your pain is my pain. I am you. You are me. There is only one. Lost and found. Forget me not!

Don't forget.

This is pure wisdom. What happens is slowly, little by little, *we forget and we re-enter the divine play.* Reminders are everywhere. Reminders that it's all play. I'm just a reminder. I remind you that it all is okay. Smile! All is well. I'm God reminding others that they're God, too.

It's just a vast divine cosmic play. But I'm under it all. I'm in it all. Sometimes I like to forget. I sleep. We all do. It's all a wild cosmic game with your Self. Peekaboo!

BREAK A LEG!

It's like a play where all the characters are hallucinating and they forgot it's only a play. For this reason, they are all taking it all very seriously. Oh, what a drama we are in, they think. But one character (you!) wakes up from the hallucination and tries to remind the others that hey, look, it's only a play.

And then, the kicker, the one awake character then realizes that it's playing every role, *all at once!*

What!

A wild paradigm shift occurs and you suddenly know that the world and everything in it *is not outside but inside!* It's inside out, or perhaps better yet, *outside in!* No church is necessary here to awaken. Only a still mind. Do it.

True wisdom is the realization that you created an imaginary universe. Wake up. Watch thoughts come and go and follow one of them and find out exactly where it came from. Down the rabbit hole you go! If you follow it deeply enough you will reach a place beyond words, just pure infinite silence.

This is pure imagination. This is You.

This was never born and never dies.

Thinking is *not* it. The mind's true state is silence and astonishment. All experience occurs against a holy backdrop of pure silence. The false self searches for anything to latch onto in the phenomenal world, and all of it, *ALL*, is only a pale substitution for the True You which is hidden underneath.

Really.

Dream Dialogue Nine (In Four Parts)

❦

PART ONE
Randi is sitting with me at a table.

Randi: (smiling, his Kris Kringle blue eyes twinkling) I've got you, Jimmy! I have THE refutation for your dream theory...

Me: Oh yeah? Isn't that cute. Psst. Hey, Randi. Wake up!

Randi: (frowns) Oh fudge!

Randi wakes up, back in his bed.

Randi: Ugh!

PART TWO
Randi begrudgingly gets out of bed and gets dressed for dinner with me. Drives over to the restaurant and takes a seat at my table.

Randi: I've got you, Jimmy! I have THE refutation for your dream theory...

Me: No you don't. Wake up, Randi. Wake up!

Randi: Oh no, this just can't beeeeeeee!

Randi wakes up, back in his bed, rubs his eyes.

Randi: DOH! Astonishing!

PART THREE
Randi begrudgingly gets out of bed and gets dressed for dinner with me. Drives over to the restaurant and takes a seat at my table.

Randi: (visibly out of breath) I've got you, Jimmy! I have a refutation for your dream theory...

Me: (smiles, waving) Sayonara! Adios, amigo! Au revoir! That's French! For wake up!

Randi: (wide eyed) Impossible!

Me: (winking) Goodbye, Old Sport!

Randi wakes up, yet again, back in his bed.

Randi: (shakes his head) I am unbelievable!

PART FOUR
Randi once again very begrudgingly gets out of bed and gets dressed for dinner with his apprentice. He drives over to the restaurant and takes a seat at my table.

Me: (looking very refreshed) Howdy!

Randi: (starts knocking on the table, checking the chair, toying with the salt shaker, not making any assumptions, seemingly checking for solidity)

Me: (eyebrow raised) Hmm...

Randi: (looking around, very aware, anxious)

Me: Question for you, Randi. How many times is it going to take for you, a skeptic of the highest order, to stop making assumptions and start doubting this place?

CHAPTER 9

Risking Everything

❦

*We are like the spider. We weave our life and then move
along in it. We are like the dreamer who dreams and then
lives in the dream. This is true for the entire universe.*

-*The Upanishads*

The Tail End of Our Astonishing Tale

Well, here we are, near the end of our journey together. Time to finish
the book and place it in The Amazing Randi's hands, a dangerous mission indeed! Each time I reminded Paul of this inevitable conclusion,
he would say, *you're a brave man.*

I was driven to write this book for one reason only and that was to
help liberate others from suffering and to point the way to the light, as
Paul had done for me. It's now time to show others their true nature and
to tell them how wrong we were about the very fabric of space and time
and to give them the astonishing news that we're all truly one and that
without a doubt, consciousness is prior to matter.

Astonishing, isn't it? Consciousness, not matter, is fundamental. To
echo the great Albert Einstein, *the world is merely an illusion, albeit an extremely powerful one.*

I'm now prepared to face my master and ready to slay that ferocious
dragon of materialism that threatens the world. The time has come

to share this experience and truth with my friends, friends who are so amazing and such skeptics and great thinkers. I can't wait to share the truth of nonduality with them and hear their thoughts and ideas about what has happened here.

First, though, I would go see my friend the incredible philosopher Raymond Smullyan. After all, he's on my side, so I can run things past him and see what he thinks before publishing the book. Next, I would see what my friend and another great philosopher, Simon Critchley, is up to. Soon after that, I will finish this book and personally put it in the hands of the brilliant Douglas Hofstadter.

Then, finally, last but certainly not least, deliver it to my teacher, my mentor, my hero and the most famous, outspoken and feared skeptic known to humankind, James Randi.

Yikes!

Of these incredible gentlemen and heavyweight minds I ask only one thing. Their job is to be skeptical and after I, James Randi's proté-gé, the skeptic's apprentice himself, who has never bullshitted them and is extremely rational and critical and who has already proven to them that he *does not believe in bullshit of any kind whatsoever,* tell them that I've found out, *for certain,* through *direct experience,* that this life we're living is truly all just a dream of separation and that really, under it all, *consciousness is eternal and never dies,* their job becomes a simple one, to investigate that extraordinary claim.

To admit that there is a chance that they too missed something, just as I did. To be absolutely honest. To look into that telescope and not flinch, just as I did. Is this too much to ask?

The payoff is eternity!

Well, we shall soon see.

THE DIFFERENCE BETWEEN KNOWLEDGE AND WISDOM
Ever since my first trip up to see philosopher Raymond Smullyan high in the beautiful Catskill Mountains of New York, I try to take

the journey a few times a year. Every time I go, I wonder, how will the Zen master be this time? Will he be as sharp? Will he be ok? Well, let me tell you, this amazing man hasn't lost a step, hasn't slipped one bit, and he's ninety six years old. Sharp as ever. Quick. Funny. Witty. Charming. Amazing!

It is now the year 2015 and I am up in the mountains visiting Raymond and I'm ready to tell him that he was right in his numerous writings about existence, that life truly is a dream. After a wonderful dinner with Raymond and friends, Raymond and I arrived back at his house where we had a wonderful talk about cosmic consciousness, about idealism, and I went into full detail all about my adventure with Paul Harris and the experience of the paradigm shift and how life truly was a dream of birth and death.

As I was speaking, I could see in Raymond's eyes that he hadn't had the experience himself, not yet anyway! I asked him point blank if he had experienced this shift and he admitted that no, he had not.

He then told me a great story from one of his favorite sages, Chuang Tzu.

Raymond said that Nan-po asked Nu-yu, Sir, you are old, but have the look of a child. How is this?

I have learned Tao, replied Nu-yu.

Can Tao be learned? Nan-po said.

Ah! How can it? replied Nu-yu. You are not the type of man. Pu-liang—I had the ability of the sage but did not know the teachings. I knew all the teachings but did not have his ability. But still I had to teach him.

It was three days before he was able to transcend this world. After he transcended this world, I waited for seven days more and then he was able to transcend all material things. After he transcended all material things, I waited for nine days more and then he was able to transcend all life.

Having transcended all life, he became as clear and bright as the morning. Having become as clear and bright as the morning, he was able to see the One. Having seen the One, he was then able to abolish the distinction of past and present.

Having abolished the past and present, he was then able to enter the realm of neither life nor death!

Raymond smiled.

I exclaimed that *that was it!*

It was very clear that Raymond grasped it intellectually, he understood it intellectually as well as anyone in the world. He said that the funny thing was that he knew exactly what cosmic consciousness was but that he was not sure he believed in what it implied, namely, consciousness being prior to matter.

I told Raymond that belief had absolutely nothing to do with this. Direct experience is what mattered here.

Raymond said he found the notion truly beautiful, but wasn't sure it was true.

I was amazed. Even the great Raymond Smullyan, the wise Zen master of the mountains of New York, hasn't experienced what I had experienced, which was exactly what the great Jack Kerouac had experienced, and the poet Allen Ginsberg, and the poet Han Shan, and the Zen master Huang Po, or DT Suzuki, Trungpa, Buddha, Lao Tzu, Marguerite Porete, Meister Eckhart, Thomas Merton, the list goes on and on. All great minds that have awoken from the dream of separation.

Just as you will, if you haven't already, my friend.

It's a great club to be a member of, The Infinity Club. If it isn't too late for Raymond, it isn't too late for you!

As those musical bodhisattvas Lennon and Harrison urged, turn off your mind and float downstream.

A LITTLE HELP FROM MY FRIENDS

While talking to Raymond, I couldn't help but think of the future conversations I would have with Douglas Hofstadter and Simon Critchley and ultimately, with Randi.

Also, I was curious what the world famous philosopher Daniel Dennett would have to say about all this. After all, he felt that he had already explained consciousness back in the early 1990's in his book aptly titled *Consciousness Explained.*

This should be fun!

Okay, back to Raymond. Here I was, thinking all along that I had Raymond in my pocket, on my side.

I didn't even have that!

Thankfully, Raymond *does* seem to side with idealism, with non-duality, but even though he's written book after book on the subject, with great delight, he's clearly not convinced. Maybe Simon will be more sympathetic to my claims? Maybe! But Dan, Doug and Randi? To say that these three giants are hardcore materialists is putting it lightly. How will I go about sharing this tremendous mind-blowing news with them?

The greatest news in the world. Will they shun me? Will they slam a door in my face? Face to face with them and trying to share the ineffable over dinner would be out of the question.

That's why the book. The plan is to finish this book and then present them (and you!) with it and meet-up after they read all about the experience.

RELAX AND SURRENDER TO THE VOID

Well, maybe just maybe, Randi will temporarily slam a door in my face, but Doug, he wouldn't do that. Randi is a world renowned curmudgeon, but Doug would be more patient, hopefully.

Will there be less phone calls, emails, and dinner invites?

Hope not. Actually, I think they might love it.

It is a risk I have to take. I have to tell them all what happened and try to get them to investigate this. It is the ultimate game changer. Perhaps coming from me, a true hardcore skeptic, perhaps they will listen.

Maybe!

As the Sufi poet Hafiz wrote, an awake heart is like a sky that pours light!

Time to light it up.

TRANSACTIONS WITH THE MOON

It will be interesting to see if I can get Douglas Hofstadter to admit that the swirling ethereal mathematical abstractions at the bottom of everything are just the same as pure imagination.

Pure imagination, possibilities, dreamt up compressed nothingness in the shape of form. What in the world will he say to *that?*

This past year I've been sharing the great Sufi poets with his beautiful and incredibly talented daughter, Monica. I took a chance one day and shared the poetry of Hafiz and Rumi and Kabir and Monica fell in love with them just as I had and we messaged each other many of these beautiful poems and discussed their non-dual philosophy and together we've built a loving friendship that means the world to me.

The Sufis are saying the same thing I am saying in this book. Life is a dream from which we must awaken. It's a divine play and there's only one player playing all of the parts. *You.* I am another you and you are another me, wrote Rumi. We're one!

What you seek is seeking you.

Hafiz urges us to become the one who lives with a full moon in each eye. The one that is always saying, with that sweet moon language, what every other eye in this world is dying to hear. Hafiz reminds us that everyone is God speaking. Why not be polite and listen?

One memorable night, the lovely Monica and I went to a restaurant and sat at an outside table and during our meal we read the Sufis to each other right there under the stars in Brooklyn and let me tell you, we spoke that sweet divine language to each other and we even made transactions with the moon.

Yes, the moon. What a night!

My phone had a low signal and I asked Monica if she thought that the restaurant might have Wifi? She wasn't sure. Well, all we need to-night is SuFi, I punned, to her delight.

Later we informed our waiter that the moon would be paying our bill. The waiter laughed heartily and enjoyed us all night and when the time came he even read us the bill as a poem!

The moon thanks you, we shouted in unison!

❦

The subject tonight is Love
And for tomorrow night as well.
As a matter of fact
I know of no better topic
For us to discuss
Until we all
Die!

-Hafiz

❦

There is nothing in this world that compares to my friend Monica reading mystical love poetry to me across a moonlit table in Brooklyn.

During our dinner her phone rang and it was her brother Danny, another good friend of mine. He tells us that he's out in the desert and that soon he's headed for the California forests to study owls. Danny told me that he started reading some Thomas Merton and that he loves solitude and that he is going to try his hand at writing haiku.

Perfect. What a dream! In a way, the Hofstadter kids are on my side, whether they know it or not.

Now on to dear old dad!

But, I'm not feeling the pressure. When you finally come to know your True Self, when you finally feel all that love, love which is the real you, you're no longer interested in fancy philosophical debate.

No, my eyes now hold the stars and galaxies and that beautiful moon. My smile reflects infinity and my silence is now holy and of eternity.

SCHOPENHAUER AND THE SALT SHAKER

A few years ago Michele and I were sitting in a restaurant across from Doug and his wonderful wife to be, (they're now married!) Baofen. I made the salt shaker disappear. Then it reappeared and Michele made it disappear. Doug said do that again! She did, and I think he started to figure out the trick. He was smiling at her, knowingly. I reached into my bag and slid a Schopenhauer book across the table to Doug. He again smiled that great Hofstadter smile and slowly slid it back to me.

Oh, he's far too pessimistic for me, Doug said.

Smiling back, I once again slid it towards him, saying yes, but not this book, not *The World as Will and Representation.* Doug smiled and slid it back, again, saying yes, pessimistic, way too pessimistic for him.

No no, I said, sliding the great Schopenhauer tome back towards him. *This* book is optimistic, this book is wonderful, and it's the answer to the tremendous mystery of life, right here, right now, under your very nose, on this table right before you!

Beautiful Baofen curiously leaned in, smiling. Michele was also smiling, excited at what we were saying. I lifted up the salt shaker and brought it down with a thud right in front of Doug Hofstadter.

You cannot know this salt shaker, Doug. You Kant know it.

Doug's smile broadened and he said, Oh sure I can! He was thinking rationally, and scientifically, of course.

No, no no, I replied, playfully waving my index finger at him, you can only know your *representation* of the salt shaker.

You absolutely Kant know *the thing in itself.* Das ding an sich! So there!

Sure I can, said Doug.

Nope, Hofstadter. You're wrong. Kant be done. Impossible!

I then launched into an explosive explanation of Schopenhauer, using Plato and Kant to back me up, just as the brilliant German philosopher had done well over a hundred years ago. I could see Baofen smiling and listening optimistically, but Doug, he sure was *pessimist* that night!

Michele would tell me later while we were driving home that she was in awe of how loose and confident I had spoken to this man that she knew I absolutely idolized for all of these years. Douglas Hofstadter was always the measuring stick of excellence that I would try to measure up to.

Now, here I was behaving salty and assaulting him with Schopenhauer, trying to shake him up!

PLATO'S CAVE

The reason Doug could not know the salt-shaker-in-itself is because, as Kant stated, we can only know the *appearance* we see, but never the true thing-in-itself. For Schopenhauer, a good way to explain this Kantian thinking was to use Plato's cave as an example and to show the difference between the thing in itself and the shadow of the real.

Kant called these two worlds the phenomenal world and the noumenal world. The appearance (phenomenal) and thing in itself (noumenal). Schopenhauer called the appearance the representation or the idea and the thing in itself the Will.

Many analogies have been used. The manifested and the unmanifested. The drop and the mighty ocean. The ripple and the serene, peaceful and very still lake.

For Schopenhauer, matter was energy down at bottom, a mere representation of the one true thing, the thing in itself, the noumenal, the one Buddha mind, the pure imagination:

Accordingly, with death consciousness is certainly lost, but not that which produced and sustained consciousness; life is extinguished, but not the principle of life also, which manifested itself in it. Therefore a sure feeling informs everyone that there is something in him which is absolutely imperishable and indestructible.

He called this *the better consciousness.*

You will die, that's for certain. Thy *hauer* will come. But something will remain. The world as your idea will cease to be, but something will remain unscathed. As Schopenhauer would say, along with all the great sages, when you die you will be what you were before you were born.

Don't misinterpret this nihilistically as nothing, because Schopenhauer meant that what you will be is your True Self, Kant's das ding an sich, the noumenal, which is outside of the limited finite grasp of time and space and impermanence and is *always* present, whether it is right now as you read this amazing sentence I'm writing to you this very moment or after your death or before you were ever born.

We like to say you entered the phenomenal world at birth, but really *the phenomenal world entered You.* We like to say we leave the phenomenal world at death, but really *the phenomenal world leaves You.*

Words, words, words, Hamlet would say. What does this all mean? It means that you don't just become Noumenal after you die. It means that whatever about you that's Noumenal *already is,* right now, at this present moment.

What Schopenhauer and I are saying is that you Kant *not* be noumenal.

You always were. Before birth, during life, and after death.

You're welcome! Bask in *that* for a while. Enjoy it.

It is the very stuff that joy is made of.

Sure, you'll lose your thoughts and memories and phenomenal self, but trust me, they're very overrated compared to das ding an sich, the one true no thing that lies outside of space and time.

LILA!

The Hindus have a terrific idea they call Lila, which means seeing the world as a divine play. Everybody and everything is in costume, veiled, but underneath those costumes, those masks (person, from persona, meaning mask), is the one thing, *the thing-in-itself.*

This thing-in-itself, the noumenal, makes an appearance and gets lost at the masquerade ball, experiencing such a phenomenal time, forgetting that it is *the host and the party goers* and *the whole show*, that it is simply seduced by its own imaginings and hallucinations.

Das Ding an sich, drunk on consciousness, as such, Kant find its way home!

Doug knows this. He said it himself, that the self is a hallucination hallucinated by a hallucination. He knows.

But he doesn't know that he knows it.

How beautiful is that! What a game of hide and seek in the void!

❦

I have free will, but not of my own choice. I have never freely chosen to have free will. I have to have free will, whether I like it or not!

-RAYMOND SMULLYAN

AT THE FEET OF THE MASTER

Okay, let's get back to Raymond Smullyan's house! I'm sitting on the floor, at the feet of the philosophy master, Dr. Smullyan, who sits in a comfortable chair in his living room, the same chair he sits in when he writes his books. He had some of his books he was presently reading scattered on the floor by the chair, mostly books on mysticism, Hinduism, and Buddhism.

The word *Upanishads* means at the feet of the master.

I soon realize it is me holding court, telling Raymond that I know it may sound crazy, but it's true, so very true, that this life is merely a dream.

And I know it. Not surmise it. Not have faith in it. Not believe it. Know it.

And I know that he can know it, too!

Raymond is intensely listening and tells me it's not crazy at all and that crazy is too strong of a word and the wrong word for it.

He says it's a wonderful idea, but he doesn't know if it's *true*. I look around me. All the books on the floor next to his writing chair were written by mystics, such as Thomas Merton, or Zen poets such as Gary Snyder, and they were all saying exactly what I was saying, which was that the world is a dream, an idea, a representation. The phenomenal world isn't the one true thing, it is held hostage by those two bitches Time and Space and that crazy kook Causality!

Okay, maybe they didn't put it quite in those terms. That was just me. But Raymond, I say, we're infinite, we really are! Just know that.

All of these people here on the floor with me are telling you that one truth and you're so very drawn to it and all of its beauty because it *is you*!

Raymond, you *are* that pure imagination beyond space and time. But not your ego, *that* has to go in order for you to know!

Raymond listened intently and smiled and countered with a barrage of jokes and anecdotes about idealism and nonduality. This made me smile, because I was seeing *right through* to the divine play itself, seeing clearly that *even Raymond Smullyan* doesn't know that he is the true one supreme consciousness itself, hiding in the mirage body of a brilliant logician who loves the ideas but just Kant believe in them.

Yet!

After all, he's only ninety six. This guy! There was still time!

The Lady or the Tiger?

Don't forget, Smullyan is the guy that Randi's very own hero, Martin Gardner, had called the *most entertaining logician and set theorist who ever lived!*

Raymond wrote the famous book, *The Lady, or the Tiger,* wherein he lays out the puzzle in which a king gives prisoners a choice between a number of doors. Behind each door was either a lady or a tiger. But the king tacks a statement on each door that is either true or false. It is then up to the prisoner to use logic to decide which door to throw open. Choose the tiger and say goodnight. Choose the lady and you're alright.

Now here I was presenting nonduality to Raymond, live and in person, and it is as if he has chosen to just read the signs but to never open a door.

That choice is as good as opening the door to the tiger. He just flat out refuses to open the door that leads to eternity, and he refuses to cleanse his doors of perception.

Sure, he admits it all could be true and that's the whole crux right there, I can get him to admit the possibility, but the next step to knowing is *the experience,* which is extremely unlikely without meditation, or without the yogi medicine, but not impossible.

So everyone just sits around staring at the eternity pill option and giving their opinions, like staring at a door, and guessing what's on the other side, versus just walking right through it and *knowing.*

Riddle me this, my friend: Behind one door is Death, ever so patiently waiting to put your lights out for good. Behind the other door Eternity awaits.

Which door will you choose?

I'm literally *pointing* to the right door; it's the one with the sign that reads "Nonduality" on it.

Throw it open! Meditate. Awaken. You now know what the game is, the jig's up, it's transparent, all is clear, exposed.

Remember, though, when others don't listen to this message, that's okay, too, because it's all a game. Have fun with it. Be creative. Play the game.

This is the only game in town. Waking yourself up *within others*! What a task!

Tease it, tickle it out of them, let them see the open window, the way out!

Anything else, *everything* else, is dream. All of it. Marvelous as it may appear to be, it's still a dream. It's only temporal. Fleeting. Evanescent. Even if you're living the American Dream, it's still just a dream. Wake up, stay awake, more and more, and then awaken your True Self in others. Don't give in to fear. Ever. Forget fear.

Remember, there is no need to convince yourself because you're already there, you're already it.

The sun doesn't need to warm itself. The sun doesn't need to illuminate itself. It already is that.

And so are you.

I'M OVER HERE NOW!

Let me try to explain this tremendous mystery best I can in words.

What happens when you let your ego dissolve is that there is a point of view switch, a flip in identity, a shift, and you fully realize and know that your true nature is not the ego, the thinker of thoughts, but the awareness that all of this *rests in*.

You see the pure imagination that dreams all of this up.

You realize that you are the Will, not the Representation.

You realize that you are the ocean, not the drop.

You realize that you are the territory, not the map.

You know that you are the meal, not the menu.

And what a meal it is!

This book is the map to that very meal, the endless meal of beauty and perfection and infinite perfect peace.

You are that. You are not your thoughts, your concepts, your ideas, your ego.

You are *not.*

What you are, when you dissolve the ego boundaries, is you are eternity itself, you are space, you are the space it all rests in, it all is you.

It's like looking out at a forest, as I am right now as I sit here outside of Raymond Smullyan's house and write this, and as you look out into the forest, you turn your gaze slowly to look within, flipping a switch on your identity, flipping from *in* the body over here in a chair typing words to *being* the mountains, the trees, the air, the chair, the person typing-

All of it, is *in You.* It *is* You.

You are it!

All of our suffering comes from not knowing this one true thing.

Suffering comes from not knowing this Truth.

This isn't magic, supernatural, occult, psychic, woo, or anything but Truth.

A true skeptic investigates this right now.

What a true skeptic does not do is pass it off as woo and move on.

An honest skeptic looks into this immediately. How could you not? Don't be so locked in your paradigm of how you think the world works and not test this.

Give it a shot. Read up on it, it's the best news ever. You are not finite. You're infinite! You're the whole deal! And then some!

So, all is alright, always, believe it or not, know it or not, but *to know this* transforms this place, removes the fear of death, and drenches existence with pure joy!

HOW TO SEE THE TRUTH FOR YOURSELF
The question to ask is can this shift to true identity happen through just silent meditation? The quick answer is, yes it can.

It might take one time, or ten times, or it might take twenty years, who knows? But it can be experienced directly.

Here is what you must do. Find a quiet place, shut the lights out, and sit quietly in silent darkness. Go within. Don't think. If thoughts come, and they will, watch them come and go, like visitors, but don't see them as *your* thoughts, don't attach to them.

Remain unattached to any thoughts or images that come. Let them come and go, like birds who land on a tree and then fly away. The tree never holds the birds there, doesn't ask for them to come visit and doesn't ask them to leave. They come and go as they please.

Be that.

Like a mirror, the tree doesn't hold the birds, just as a mirror doesn't hold an image, it just reflects it. Like a lake with the moon in it or a dew drop with the sun in it. Don't attach, don't hold.

Just let go of everything, let go of your whole story. All of it.

I have traded my four Master Degrees for a Doctorate in Detachment.

TOOLS TO ENLIGHTENMENT

If after a while you can't do this and it isn't working for you, maybe take a little puff of something, this will help you relax the TMF and allow a break through, a piercing of the noumenal.

For those who really need some more help, mdma can be used, although unfortunately this is presently illegal here in the USA.

Of course, something that dissolves the prison of the ego is made illegal by the government. But if you can get your hands on this and you take it as described above, in silent darkness, the brief four hour journey it takes you on will be the path to astonishment and to your True Self.

Again, this is *not* to be taken recreationally, but during quiet meditation wherein you let go of everything. Total surrender.

Haven't you had enough re-creation? Re-presenting?

Go for creation itself.

Das ding an sich!

Enough with the recreational. It gets you nowhere in the end.

A good thing to meditate on is this:

If you were dreaming at night, how would you exit a dream if you figured out that your dream was just a dream?

Answer: By not believing in it. By waking up in it. By being lucid.

Do it.

THE BIG BANG THEORY

Consider this analogy Doug Hofstadter once offered. He asked us to imagine his beloved father, who had died some years ago, walking into his study one night as he was busy working. Would he not be overcome with joy? What would that astonishing event do to Doug's belief system? Everything that he had understood about the world (much of it taught to him by his father) would go down the drain in a flash. Death would cease to exist and basically everything he knew about biology and the other sciences would be wrong.

Would he, Douglas Hofstadter, want to trade the joy of having his father back for the destruction of his entire belief system? Doug said he would in fact *not* welcome such an event.

What will Doug say to me when he reads all about my paradigm shift? What will he say when I inform him just how close his brilliant ideas are to the truth? How will he react when I exuberantly tell him that his lifelong and relentless pursuit of beauty is really a search for his *own true nature*, which *is* endless beauty and love its very self?

This is the guy who at dinner, when I made a tiny model of a human brain vanish into thin air, magically, with sleight of hand...only to have Doug spot it seconds later, rolling quietly away from my lap across the restaurant floor, quipped to me:

James, that trick was a *no brainer..*!

Once when Michele was seeing a production of the play, Shakespeare's Twelfth Night, she texted me from her seat at the play, anxious to join me, Doug and Monica, at a restaurant where we were having drinks and appetizers. She texted that the play was almost over and she would be joining us soon.

I informed Doug, who quickly said, with a big smile, eyes shining: James, *it's the eleventh hour of the Twelfth Night!*

This is the guy who penned the book *Gödel, Escher, Bach: An Eternal Golden Braid.* My favorite book. A book that changed my life!

The guy who declared, in print, as mentioned above, that if his own deceased father miraculously appeared in his study and said Hey Doug, look, we were all wrong about the universe and about death- would rather that *not* to happen, because he'd rather his materialist views be right because his ideas not only shaped who he was but *were who he was* and if he and his ideas were wrong, well, he would crumble to dust.

When I first read that, I was astonished. How could you not want to see your father again, I thought? But the younger materialist me applauded Doug for what he said because I thought it was brave.

But now?

Now I say let it crumble you, Doug. You only think you are your ideas. But you're *much much more than that!*

Doug already knows that there is no such thing as a self. He is the main reason "I" never believed in a self. His ideas convinced me long ago that the self was a fiction. Buddhism and Doug and many other great thinkers, such as Daniel Dennett, Patricia Churchland, Derek Parfit, all convinced me of this. Thomas Metzinger wrote a great book called *Being No One.* In the book he clearly states that there never was a self, ever. That the self is only an illusion. Many great minds know this intellectually. Doug knows this intellectually. So do "I".

But now?

Now I've *confirmed* it. Now, the knowing is from within. Not merely in words or theory, but in reality. Absolute knowledge.

This is Prajnaparamita. Pure wisdom. Talk about a *no brainer..*! Whew.

Sitting in Raymond's yard, I just watched a deer walk quietly past, a beautiful brown bunny hop on by, and a bird, one with bright blue feathers, fly in and out of the untouched forest. Watched this all with child-like eyes, as if *truly seeing* for the very first time.

As if that isn't enough, then the point of view shifts and I now know that I *am* the birds, the forest, the deer, the bunny. The whole eternal show. I'm all of it, it all is made *of* me and rests *in* me.

The world is my idea. And your's too! We are one. For real.

How to Convince Doug and Randi

I decided to make a list of things I would say to Doug and Randi when, after reading this book, we meet face to face. The first would be to describe the shift in identity, the shift in point of view. Next, I would discuss the nature of a dream. Explain exactly how a dream works and use it as an analogy.

Then, discuss how matter is *empty*. How the self is an *illusion*. Try to describe to them, firmly, exactly what happens when all thought is dropped and one stays in silence and the present moment. Explain how that matches every other sage throughout the history of thought and how it matches up beautifully with Kant's idea of the noumenal.

I'd explain imagination and the nature of the *seduction* by its very *own* imaginings.

Importantly, I will make it clear that nonduality is still a monist position; there's only *one* kind of stuff in the universe, and it's *consciousness*, and consciousness is prior to the appearance of matter.

A major point I need to convey to these two amazing gentlemen is that they should not forget that I, too, *am a skeptic,* as skeptical as Randi himself.

With that said, this experience is *very real.*

Surely one of them will call it a hallucination. Or some brain state.

How will they explain the complete transformation I've gone through, losing my fear of death, all the joy it has brought with it, this knowing eternity itself?

Key point: How do I make sure Randi doesn't call in the folks with the straightjackets? Or get mad at me? Or just not listen?

Doug, I imagine will listen. But Randi?

This is a guy with a business card that states his name, James Randi, and then there are just two words under it, describing him:

Curmudgeon
Iconoclast

Seriously. This is The Amazing Randi we're talking about now. This is no joke. He's no pussycat. His doorbell basically says you had better bring it or don't ring it.

Must be ready!

DON'T FORGET, LILA!

See, for a second there I forgot that this is *all just play*. I took it seriously, rather than experiencing it as divine play where the one true thing is hiding and seeking and playing peekaboo with the everything and everything is playing peekaboo back because there's only one thing, pure imagination. Forgot!

A question just popped up in my head. If I had a dream and in that very dream I was going to meet with Randi and try to convince him that nonduality is the meaning of life, how would I go about that in the most convincing way, where he actually listens and wonders if what I am saying may in fact be true or not?

How, in a dream, would you convince someone else in the very same dream that it was all just a dream?

Ah, therein lies *the rub...*

Maybe write a book about it, saying meditation in silence is the key.

Hey, are we having any fun yet?

I really hope you're having as much fun reading this as I am writing it!

Another question just occurred to me, just popped up. A question for Doug and Randi.

How does it feel to have *me*, a true skeptic, bringing you this message that *life is all a dream?*

Who Are You?

The feeling in life you get from beauty is really what *you* truly *are*, it's you. The feeling love gives you, the warmth, *is* what *you are*. You *are* goodness, love, peace, oneness, wholeness, and *you are* endless. The feeling of timelessness is wonderful because it's what *you are*. You are that. The feeling of happiness is so pleasurable and sought out because it's what *you are*, you're trying to go home, and you're trying to be whole again, to wake up from the dream of being separate. It's so simple. Knowing this, you're drenched in joy.

Convincing Raymond

If even Raymond Smullyan isn't convinced, how am I ever going to convince James Randi?

At times, this just seems like an impossible task. I mean, Raymond has written books on this and has read everything from Bucke's Cosmic Consciousness to Suzuki and Watts and Buddha and Lao Tzu.

And even he isn't totally buying it. Unless...unless he's just pulling my leg. Being a Zen prankster. Maybe he's bluffing!

After all, it's all a cosmic poker game and maybe he just doesn't want me to see all of his cards.

This book ensures you that all of my cards are on the table. Nonduality is true and you and I are infinite. That's just a fact and I'm here to inform you of it.

But maybe that's not enough? Maybe I need to play the game, raise the stakes and try to win, and convince him, so that he wins, too.

A bodhisattva convinces others of the truth, wakes up others knowing they are all one thing that forgot its true nature.

There are times I don't want to play the game. I just want to watch it all unfold, knowing all is okay always and forever.

But, then you see others suffering unnecessarily, and you want to lend a hand, want to assure them all is truly alright.

Which it is.

Know that, dear reader.

If it isn't true, then I have never written and you have never read.

Shakespeare! One smart cat!

RE-ENTERING THE FRAY

So yeah, sometimes I don't want to play, sometimes I just don't want to try, I just want to sit back and enjoy the show. But all that suffering, although only illusory in the big picture, forces my hand, makes me enter the game and play, and raise the stakes, from finity to infinity.

How can one not want to try this?

Investigate it and attempt it. Even if you think it's a brain state, *it's one hell of a state to be in*, one of pure joy and happiness, perfect peace and total transformation. I say roll the dice!

ASTONISHMENT THEATER

What a beautiful play this glorious existence really is! Raymond Smullyan is one of the most brilliant thinkers on the planet and he knows nonduality inside and out. He's passionately and joyfully driven to publish book after book on it. But even he hasn't experienced it himself. Even *he* isn't sure that it is true.

Then you have Douglas Hofstadter. *Greatest mind since Einstein!* Doug chases after beauty his whole life. He pursues wholeness, complex word play, bon mots, and self referentiality. Why? Because it is all *who he truly is* and he just wants to be himself, find himself, know himself, but ... he doesn't know it!

Doug Hofstadter once said that he found in reductionism the ultimate religion. That his lifelong training in physics gave him a very deep awe when seeing how the seemingly most substantial and familiar objects and experiences *fade away* when one approaches the i*nfinitesimal* scale and they become an eerily insubstantial ether, a myriad of ephemeral swirling vortices of incomprehensible mathematical activity. He said that this evoked in him a feeling of cosmic awe and mystery.

Question: How is THAT any different than pure imagination?

Answer?

It isn't!

The skeptical Amazing Randi himself says it's a theory that might be true, but that it cannot be verified. Well I'm saying it *has* been verified by me, his student, and by countless others and all of the reports match, so what do you have to say about that?

Maybe, just maybe, it's all part of the game, a game which the TMF just won't quit. It's in its nature to be here and enjoy the ride, so it cannot and will not see the truth. It refuses to see behind the mask and it sticks with fairytales, desire and pleasure. It must do this or die.

What a wild game to play!

I'm reminded of the ending of one of Raymond's books where he wrote the following:

I still sometimes have the haunting feeling that I am overlooking something crucial, that I may be missing something of extreme importance. How can I find it? God only knows! There is nothing more at present that I can possibly do. But who knows? Maybe one day the idea, if there really is any idea, might dawn on me. Perhaps through further advance of science, through a more refined logical analysis of the question, or through something like a sudden mystical insight, it might happily happen that I will say, "Ah, of course! How simple! So that's what reality really is!"

Perfect! That's exactly it! Don't miss it!

It's a mass hallucination. A mass delusion. But one wherein the nonduality theory looks like the hallucination or the delusion! It almost sounds absurd to flip it and say that life is actually a dream and that you are pure imagination seduced by its own imaginings.

What a game of hide and seek, peekaboo, tag, *you're it.*

It's self reference taken to the *extreme*, it is what everything points to, and it all is pointing at itself. It's all one big finger pointing; not at the moon, but at itself. It's one big Godelian finger, a finger so big that even Kurt Gödel and Hofstadter and Smullyan aren't making that last leap up. Unless, of course, I can convince them.

What an adventure together as one in the jam packed void!

Effing Up the Ineffable

Here's the teaching, one last time, plain and simple:

You forgot who you truly are. I'm just reminding you. Reminding you that all is well, always and forever. Not only that, but, despite all appearances, you aren't just a temporal mind trapped in a finite skin bag that will someday turn cold and die.

You're the whole show. The whole ball of wax. The whole shebang.

There is no birth, so there is no death, life is a dream, and you simply forgot this and now you're caught in the dream of separation from yourself, your True Self, which is always bliss.

The dream, the ego, the shadow - the little you that you think you are- suffers because it is lost and it needs to get back home.

A more beautifully elegant and simple idea than this does not exist.

Want some more astonishment?

Everything you see or hear or sense in any way is just a sign pointing you towards home or directing you away from home and locking you back into the dream. Everything is either pointing towards the noumenal or towards the phenomenal dream world.

But, remember, all signs are, at bottom, noumenal.

Everything is made of pure imagination, pure consciousness, and everything is a clue to help you find your True Self.

The great Ram Dass once said that we're all walking one another home.

He was right!

That's the teaching.

So, in this life whenever you find yourself feeling sad, think of this, read these words, and know deep down that all is okay.

But, *to truly know,* you will have to directly experience this True Self. You're like the caterpillar now, which is great. But soon you are to be the butterfly. Don't cling to the cocoon, which is the world, the dream.

So, what to do?

Well, love one another, obviously. For they *are* you. Simple! Be nice. Be nice to yourself. Sometimes you/they forget. When that happens there is suffering.

Realize who you are and suffering ends. This suffering can be a teacher, too, forcing one to drop the dream. Suffering can force one to let go, to renounce the world. Suffering can make one feel like giving up.

This is a good thing, because you are not that, that's all ego, all dream talk, and when you drop it and you realize "you" truly are not...

...then your true face appears and suffering vanishes, and you see and experience the fact that it never was, it was just like a bad dream.

Then the world becomes lighter. By light here I do not mean literally light, blazing, rather light here means clear, it means shining, an illumination, a knowing like the sun.

Also you will *feel* light, weightless, and here weightlessness doesn't mean you float off the ground, that's impossible.

Rather, this weightlessness or lightness is akin to you not feeling any burden anymore.

The burden of the body, of decay, of time and space and finiteness will have been lifted and you will feel only full of peace and purity.

⚭

Dream Dialogue
Ten

⤜⤐

Randi: So, what exactly are you trying to say, Jimmy?

Me: I'm saying that in complete silence, during meditation, there is this no-state state that arises, a state of nothingness where the illusory self is dropped and the true moment is realized and seen for what it really is, eternal, and that the idea of a "you" as a separate self vanishes, the ego illusion is banished and all there is left is your true nature, which is ever present awareness, pure imagination, a knowing, a bearable lightness of being, a supreme consciousness, an omniscience- you are all, which is nothing and everything.

Life is seen to be a dream, an entanglement in an idea of this appears in this stuff called matter and a self and once this is experienced "you" are liberated, "you" are free, free from the dream of separation, of a body, a brain, an ego or a self. What's left is just infinite vastness, pure love. This is where people got the idea of heaven from.

Randi: I must admit, it sure sounds heavenly...

Me: It is heaven, Randi. Nirvana means extinction, extinction of the idea that there exists a separate you. It is oneness, wholeness, endless perfect peace.

And it's true. So stick THAT in your pipe and smoke it.

Randi: Jimmy, I don't doubt that you have had this wonderful experience.

Me: I have had it, Randi, and ALL the great sages confirm it, the very same experience.

Randi: But, how do we know if this isn't just a hallucination?

Me: You're a hallucination. You yourself are a hallucination hallucinated by a hallucination!

Randi: Hofstadter!

Me: Yes! There is no "I".

Randi: Well, "I" still need verification...

Me: I'm giving you it, man. The star student of the greatest skeptic in the world is saying we missed this. Almost!

Everything I've said is true. Life IS a dream and we are merely dream characters.

But the real You is untouchable, bottomless, endlessly true infinite peace.

PS: You're welcome! (smiles)

Randi: Jimmy, I'm very intrigued, but I need more verification.

Me: Sure, just look into the telescope...

Randi: But...

Me: Take a chance.

Randi: I...

Me: Don't be afraid, ever.

Randi: I...

Me: What have you got to lose, but your imaginary idea of your finite self?

And to gain? To know you are not really ephemeral, not mortal, but rather boundless love beyond space and time.

Randi: I...

Me: Psst...Wake up, Randi. Wake up.

Randi wakes up in a cold sweat.

He then slowly sits up in his bed, in lotus position, and closes his eyes. He is very still.

He remains this way for hours.

✎

CHAPTER 10

Face to Face

❧

MYSTICISM 401

RECENTLY, I WROTE SIMON CRITCHLEY to tell him that I was writing a book about the mystical experience and my paradigm shift away from materialism into nonduality. I asked Simon if we could meet up for drinks and talk about it and he congratulated me on the book and said yes let's get together as soon as possible. I had also asked about what he was teaching, so he sent me his two course outlines. I opened up the file and noticed that one was for a course on Heidegger.

Would you care to take a guess as to what the other course was on? Go ahead, guess.

Yep.

Mysticism!

Simon Critchley was teaching a course on mysticism and the mystical experience.

Come on! Knock it off. How could this be? From the book *Very Little, Almost Nothing* to Mysticism 401! From hardcore atheism to nonduality, just like me! I looked at the books they would be reading and the people he would discuss. There were the writings of Marguerite Porete and Meister Eckhart and all of the others. All saying the same thing as me.

Marguerite Porete said we must *hack and hew* a space within us big enough to let the love enter, to let the True Self enter.

Lose the false self, empty the self out. Same story. Same experience.

The only difference is that these were mystics and I am the apprentice of the most famous skeptic to ever walk upon the earth.

Everything else is the same. Nonduality is true. Questions ran through me. Had Simon moved over to nonduality too? Or was he just interested in the subject? If so, why? Why now? I couldn't wait to find out! Maybe his close friendship with the incredible philosopher Cornel West played a role?

Go West, Young Man

Did I tell you I met this man? The remarkable Dr. Cornel West? Now here was a guy who was on fire, like me. Still is. He blazed his way through the hallways of Harvard University and although he earned his PhD in philosophy many years ago, he is still very much burning away.

Is there anyone who speaks as eloquently as Cornel West?

One night I sat front row and watched Brother West debate Simon Critchley at The New School in NYC. The topic was death. Of course. Simon got up and spoke about death in a way only Simon can. I loved every word. He delivered big-time.

Then, when his turn came, Cornel West arose from his seat on stage and approached the podium. The man had no notes. He came empty handed. I said, this guy isn't going to just wing it, is he? In front of this crowd?

Well, ladies and gentlemen, wing it he did. Beautifully. He soared on those wings and he blew us all away, Simon included. I had tears in my eyes by the end of his speech. Dr. West blew the room up. Standing ovation!

When I met him years later in Brooklyn, I was with my best friend Richard and together we three talked about everything from the Gnostics to John Coltrane and then I asked if he'd like to see some magic.

Cornel smiled widely and said sure and rubbed his hands together and I produced a deck of cards and went right into a whirlwind of wild flourishes and one handed cuts and finger flinging flips and then had him pick a card. Just as I had done to Ginsberg, I shot a card out of the very well shuffled deck in my right hand high into the air and it soared into a wide arc and landed gracefully like a butterfly in my left hand.

Cornel looked at me and Richard wide eyed and said No, no, no. No, can't be, can't be. Just can't be! Can't be mine! I slowly turned it over.

Now the only way I know for a fact that it indeed was his card that had flown up high out of the deck into my waiting other hand was because Dr. West had run away.

When I say he ran, I don't mean he backed up some in amazement. No. I mean the brother ran as fast as he could to the back of the room and then turned around to face me.

Thirty feet away is being conservative. It was pure astonishment. He was shaking a finger at me and saying, No you didn't. No, no. Oh no, you didn't just do that!

Well Richard and I loved it. We were smiling back and I said, Oh yes I did. I did do that. You saw it. That just happened!

I told him that was for rocking me with his incredible books, that was for *unhousing* me time and time again with those great books, Cornel West. That's for blowing me away in your lecture on death, too.

He came back to me slowly and skeptically and shook my hand happily. Smiling that great smile. If you haven't seen Dr. West's smile, please google it. Pure joy!

Then he signed one of his books to me:

Dear Brother James,

We unhouse each other!

Stay strong!

Love, Brother West

CORNEL GOES NUTS

I didn't think I'd see him again that night, but later on, at the after party, I saw him approaching me. He cautiously walked across the room, once again shaking his finger at me as if to say, I'm watching you, my Brother James. I quickly grabbed two peanuts from a bowl on the bar and prepared to do what my good friend Johnny Wink had me do with a pair of dice in an elevator at the Doubletree Hotel in Arkansas to a behemoth of a man from the Little Rock football team that messed up said behemoth for a week! I asked Cornel to hold out his hands, wide open. He did it. I placed one peanut in his left hand and one in his right. I asked him which one he liked best.

He raised his left palm. Rich jumped in and said, He's going with the cashew! Brother Cornel is going with the cashew!

I smiled. Then, just like that, I made the cashew vanish right before Dr. West's wide astonished eyes!

He screamed. The brother screamed out in delight!

Suddenly both of his hands shot up my sleeves searching for the vanished cashew. Brother West was determined to find it up there somewhere.

Alas, of course, he came up empty. It was gone.

I then said, Watch this, Cornel! I made a magical gesture and suddenly the cashew reappeared magically in the other hand, alongside the other peanut. Together again at last.

I then asked Cornel West to please let go of my sleeves. He did. We all laughed. *Unhoused him once again.*

I wonder what Cornel West would have to say about the true astonishment I wrote about here in this book?

Not the astonishment of a clever magic trick which *temporarily* reveals one's true nature, but the *true astonishment* one attains only during deep silent meditation where there is a popping of one's paradigm and a subtle shifting from thinking you are merely finite to knowing your true nature, that you *are* eternity itself.

Would Brother West run from *that* news? I wonder. How about Brothers Hofstadter and Randi? Hmm?

Will they both run and hide from the truth? Or will they stay firmly put and investigate this like the true skeptics they claim to be?

I strongly believe it will be the latter.

Enough speculation, let's find out. Time to wrap up this book and put it in their hands. So glad it found its way into your hands, too, my dear reader!

Before I go, Raymond Smullyan told me this joke. I think it's my favorite joke of his. May I share it? May I?

A philosopher once had the following dream.

First Aristotle appeared, and the philosopher said to him, Could you give me a fifteen-minute capsule sketch of your entire philosophy?

To the philosopher's surprise, Aristotle gave him an excellent exposition in which he compressed an enormous amount of material into a mere fifteen minutes. But then the philosopher raised a certain objection which Aristotle couldn't answer. Confounded, Aristotle disappeared.

Then Plato appeared. The same thing happened again, and the philosophers' objection to Plato was the same as his objection to Aristotle. Plato also couldn't answer it and disappeared.

Then all the famous philosophers of history appeared one-by-one and our philosopher refuted every one with the same objection.

After the last philosopher vanished, our philosopher said to himself, I know I'm asleep and dreaming all this. Yet I've found a universal refutation for all philosophical systems! Tomorrow when I wake up, I will probably have forgotten it, and the world will really miss something!

With an iron effort, the philosopher forced himself to wake up, rush over to his desk, and write down his universal refutation. Then he jumped back into bed with a sigh of relief.

The next morning when he awoke, he went over to the desk to see what he had written.

It was, "That's what you say!"

RANDI AT THE HOSPITAL

According to my calculations, Randi will be eighty eight years old in 2016. I'm about half his age and I'm not kidding when I tell you that he could probably have beat me in a foot race up until maybe ten years ago. Only recently has Randi slowed down and he's slowed down just a bit.

He's using a cane, wielding it like a lightsaber now and then when the situation calls for it. He's recently beaten cancer, a battle my sweet mother lost. During my mom's radiation and chemotherapy treatments, there was Randi on Skype in her kitchen cheering her on, telling her how the chemo wasn't a nightmare for him and that helped, his encouraging words always inspired her.

The guy is a fighter. He fought against the psychics, the con artists, the faith healers- his whole life.

Now he's in a fight against time. And so are you.

Not too long ago, Randi almost died. He was on the operating table and we very nearly lost him. During this time he had a revelation on that hospital table.

He experienced something!

Something powerful happened, so extraordinary that Randi somehow had the energy and the awareness to request a pen and paper and he furiously scribbled down this secret information granted to him on what was almost his deathbed! After the operation was over, Randi awoke and asked for the paper he had written on. When he held it in his hands, ready to learn what he had been given in a flash of revelation while in the merciless grip of Death itself, Randi couldn't believe his eyes. The handwriting was too messy to read! The message couldn't be deciphered!

It is my hope that Randi finds *my* message clear. Every word of it is true. All of it.

Randi, get this. Whatever astonishing experience you had on that hospital table that day is not illusory.

The hospital is!

That light you see at the end of the tunnel is not an illusion.

It's the tunnel that's the illusion!

What you experienced on that hospital table is what I experienced the night of my awakening.

True astonishment. An enlightening flash of Truth.

I am the knight of that very same light.

Amazing, wasn't it, Randi? You realized consciousness doesn't reside in the brain after all! *You realized the brain resides in consciousness!* You realized that what You are is pure awareness. Pure imagination imagining it's an individual. A no brainer indeed!

Randi, the fiercest fuck there is, experienced this. But forgot.

See, Randi, Martin Gardner was no slouch when it came to skepticism yet he knew this.

Death is the biggest lie there is. Don't believe it. Consciousness never goes away!

A true genius is one who sees through death.

Don't miss it again.

It's what you scribbled down in that hospital bed that was undecipherable.

This.

This book and this message is the real cure, the true chemotherapy.

This and only this is permanent.

Randi, you had a flash of Truth. Waking up fully is staying on the side of eternity, not going back to the ego. It's movement from false self to false self to false self to non-self and then finally to True Self.

All the clues are there, hidden in all of the other selves and the world.

This whole worldly dream is just a playground of memory loss.

Who are you?

Truly?

You're pure consciousness! Pure imagination...

Martin knew this was true. He knew it had to be true. Unamuno, Schopenhauer, Buddha, Christ, Lao Tzu, Kerouac, Ginsberg, Meister Eckhart, they and countless others knew it too.

And so do I.

Martin felt more comfortable believing consciousness was eternal and you easily accepted this. You even celebrated it, remember?

As you would say, "Hey, if it improved Martin's life, it improved my life, too."

Martin Gardner was right. Again.

My hope is that now Randi will investigate my claims and be fiercely skeptical of them. I think he will.

That's my Randi. I expect no less.

Oh, and Randi? And reader? Now that you have come this far...

Psst.

Wake up.

CHAPTER 11

The End of Endings

SPEAKING TO YOU FROM THE POINT OF VIEW OF ETERNITY

RIGHT NOW I AM BURSTING into existence as a beautiful flower. Now I am a poor, starving child. Now I am a bird soaring high through the sky.

Right now I am that very sky. I am the corpse at the funeral. I am the weeping widow. I am her tears.

I am the not knowing. I am the full knowing. I am knowing knowing itself. I am all things. Right now.

At any given moment I flash in and out of existence. Right now I am being born and right now I am dying.

Now I am the moon shining high in the sky. Now I am the canopy of stars. I am the bursting supernova. I am the faraway galaxies twinkling beyond.

Right now I am the hungry homeless man feeding the hungry birds. I am the man. I am the birds. I am the seeds. I am the hunger.

I am war and I am peace. Ignorance and wisdom. I am the anger in this stranger's face. I am the joy in this stranger's heart.

I am all there is and all there ever was. At any given moment I flash in and out of existence.

I am the reminder that you are here, that you never left, that you have only forgotten.

Wake up and remember.

At every given moment I flash in and flash out of existence. At any moment I am born and I am dying. You cannot NOT see me. Feel me. Touch me. Taste me.

I am every wall and every opening.

I am every birth and every death.

I am all appearances, so that I may show you that you never disappear.

You, too, are always here. You never left.

You have only forgotten.

For I am always here and I am everything.

And I am you and you are me.

Don't forget.

This is a message from the now.

From your True Self.

All is well.

You are it.

This book is all about consciousness. But the real work will be done by you alone in silence. This book just points out the way. Silence is the real teaching.

True liberation is a letting go of everything, a letting go of your entire story. It is all a fabrication of time, space and appearance, all ignorance and invention, an ephemeral shadow play in the world of form.

Stay in the stillness, in the beingness and soon the arising and falling thoughts will eventually stop. It's all about keeping extremely still and quiet. It is not knowledge of things, but pure being. This being in itself is the knowing. It is the true you.

Soon you will have a realization, you will see that what you are is what makes all this experiencing, and you will see that you are not the experiencer.

Now, unattached, you jump out of the system and view it from outside of itself. You realize you are no longer a certain person, born of certain parents, who works a certain job, has responsibilities to do this or

that. A peace washes over. You are not only at peace, *you are peace itself.*
The jig is up, finally, and you see for the first time that all is well, always.

Now there is no fear. There is only love.

You are this love.

Fear of death vanishes, you have already died to the world of appearances. Now instead of a cloak of fear, you wear the universe as your very own, it is now your clothing, and it is not only freeing, but it is freedom itself.

You are now pure imagination its very self, the seduction of the world of objects and appearances is over and there remains what always was, only bliss, only joy.

This joy, this bliss, is just you finally coming home to your True Self, you finally finding and knowing your true nature now that the phantom dream of being a separate self has collapsed and you're infinitely basking in all of your never-ending pure radiance, true beauty and wholeness.

Welcome to the end of endings.

A happy ending, indeed.

"Suicide" at the Drop of a Hat!

Learn to kill thy false self on command. At the drop of a hat. When this shift in consciousness occurs, you now know that the phenomenal world is not real. You now know why most people, including your old self were blind to the target, to the noumenal.

It is because there are veils covering it. The TMF. The tenacious ego. It is because of the ego that the world seems real. Under the spell of the ego, you Kant see the target that the genius or the contemplative sees. But once you do see it, it becomes the only thing you can be a part of.

Why? Because it is true love. True beauty. Once this is truly seen the mystic must flee the fleeting world of shadows and be with the True

Self. Thoughts come and go, but awareness gently drops down to what does not come or go because it is beyond the mind.

It is the ever-present light of pure imagination. It is beyond all that chatter in your monkey mind.

Gradually the mystic clears the path of all temporal matters and just spends time communing with the eternal, the noumenal, with pure imagination itself. Looking back over a shoulder at the world, the mystic sees it now bathed in the light of pure imagination, but the mystic's eye is now and forever fixed on eternity.

All is crystal clear and the world of shadow and change pales in comparison to the one true no thing. Then there is the astonishing realization that absolutely nothing exists without this.

Without pure imagination. Without You.

Desire is gone, except that which touches on the noumenal and there is a desire to share all of this, even though at times it seems impossible!

But that's okay, because this is who you truly are and you now know this, in silence, in stillness.

Don't forget that though there appear to be appearances which seem like reality, none of this happens without You. You are ever-present pure imagination. Pure awareness.

You have cut out the ego, hacked and hewed a space for love to enter and now you're left with only pure heart.

There is a saying:

Lokah Samasta Sukhino Bhavantu: May all beings be happy and free.

May all of my thoughts, my words and my actions contribute in some way to the happiness and joy of all beings.

www.ingramcontent.com/pod-product-compliance
Lightning Source LLC
Chambersburg PA
CBHW021401090426
42742CB00009B/948